12.⁰⁰

A Multitude of Blessings

A Multitude of Blessings

A Christian Approach
to Religious Diversity

CYNTHIA M. CAMPBELL

Westminster John Knox Press
LOUISVILLE • LONDON

Scripture quotations from the New Revised Standard Version of the Bible are copyright © 1989 by the Division of Christian Education of the National Council of the Churches of Christ in the U.S.A. and are used by permission.

Book design by Drew Stevens
Cover design by Eric Walljasper, Minneapolis, MN
Cover photograph: © Régis Bossu/Sygma/Corbis

First edition
Published by Westminster John Knox Press
Louisville, Kentucky

This book is printed on acid-free paper that meets the American National Standards Institute Z39.48 standard. ∞

PRINTED IN THE UNITED STATES OF AMERICA

07 08 09 10 11 12 13 14 15 16—10 9 8 7 6 5 4 3 2 1

Library of Congress Cataloging-in-Publication Data is on file at the Library of Congress, Washington, D.C.

ISBN-13: 978-0-664-22956-6
ISBN-10: 0-664-22956-5

Contents

Preface

What is a Christian to make of religious diversity? How does one affirm faith in Jesus Christ and seek to live according to the teachings of Christian faith and at the same time live with neighbors who are not Christian? These are not new questions that people of faith find themselves asking, but they present themselves with new urgency in today's world. As we all know, the religious life of humankind is old indeed, perhaps as old as human consciousness. Long before there were Christians, people composed hymns to God giving praise for light and life; they followed the law of Moses and the teachings of the Buddha; they patterned their lives on the five relationships of Confucius. The diversity of religious life and the variety of ways in which humans have named and responded to the Holy are not new. What is new is that all of us on this planet are now more aware of this diversity. It can be argued that we now live closer to the religious lives of others than in any other era of history. Religious diversity is a factor in everyday life in our neighborhoods and schools, in the workplace and in our own families. Tragically, conflict between persons of different religious faiths and conflict in which religion plays a role are before us almost daily in the news.

This book is written for Christians who are concerned to make sense of this challenge of living with religious diversity. For the most part, I will not be talking about other religious traditions, the ways they approach reality and understand God, or the moral claims they make; this is not a book about "comparative religions." Also, I am not going to survey the variety of ways in which Christians have approached religious diversity. What I will do is present one way that Christians can think about this topic from the standpoint of our faith tradition.

Unfortunately the dominant voices responding to this situation in which we find ourselves provide answers that are less than satisfying. From some leaders of the Christian faith, all we hear is the message that Christianity is the only "true" religion. All others are "false" and those who follow them will be barred from enjoying true life with God, both now and in the life to come. These Christians marshal support from the Bible and traditional Christian teaching to support their views. The case they make seems strong indeed. But for many other Christians, this way of thinking seems to define Christianity in a very narrow way. In addition, it fails to make sense of what their own experience tells them about the moral and spiritual integrity of neighbors, friends, and family members who follow other religions.

Another strong voice comes from the other end of the spectrum. According to this view, religion should remain an entirely private matter. When it enters public life, some claim, it simply becomes part of the problem of negotiating contemporary human life, a difficulty to be overcome. If public differences over religion simply went away and all followed rational, ethical principles, humanity could find its way to peace and prosperity. Thus, one way to reduce conflict in society is to make sure that religious differences play no role in civic or political life. This view reduces religion to the realm of private feeling. One might choose to be religious or not, just as one might prefer Mozart to hip-hop, or vice versa.

For people of faith, for Christians and others, such a view of religious faith and practice is simply unacceptable. It trivializes beliefs and practices that people hold dear and that they rightly think give meaning, purpose, and direction to their lives, not only individually but as communities and in their families. Making religion a matter of personal taste or preference ignores the fact that religious people believe that their faith makes claims about the true nature of reality and about the proper foundation for human conduct and values.

How do Christians who trust in God and believe that God has called them to follow Jesus Christ in their daily lives, who believe that religious beliefs really do "matter," and who want to treat people of all religious backgrounds with respect account for the reality of religious diversity? Some years ago, a noted Christian scholar of the world's religions put it this way: "How does one account theologically for the fact of humanity's religious diversity? . . . We explain the fact that the Milky Way is there by the doctrine of creation, but how do we explain the fact that the Bhagavad Gita is there?"[1] How do we account *theologically* for the continuing existence and vitality of the world's religions? Or to put it another way, how does the religious diversity of humankind figure within the divine plan?

These are the questions that this book seeks to explore. As I will argue in the first chapter, this is first and foremost a *theological* question. It is part of who we as Christians understand God to be and how we believe that God is related to the world. Because this is a theological problem, it must be approached theologically. This means that we will look primarily at the Bible and Christian theological traditions for answers. In chapters 2, 3, and 4, I will explore various aspects of the question of religious diversity in the Bible by looking particularly at how the Bible portrays what I am calling the religious "others," that is, those who are not part of the covenant family of God's people. In this exploration, I do not seek to ignore the places in the Bible that present an "exclusive" understanding of God's revelation or that demand loyalty to that God alone. What I do hope to show is that there is a broader context within which the exclusive claims of Christian faith can be understood. In the final chapter, I will present some of the practical implications for Christian faith and life that I believe flow from a more generous understanding of God's relationship to all people.[2]

The "Brief Statement of Faith" of the Presbyterian Church (U.S.A.) says that God "makes everyone equally in God's image—male and female, of every race and people—to live as one community" and that God calls Christians "to work with others for justice, freedom and peace."[3] When we consider both what religious diversity means for Christians and how we might live with it, these affirmations will serve as the context for the conversation. If people from all races and cultures are equally created in the divine image, and if God's desire is that all live together in a world community marked by justice, freedom, and peace, then there must be room for a positive appreciation of the diversity of human religious as well as cultural life. How Christians can do this and live out our confession that Jesus Christ is both Savior and Lord is the theological question that this book seeks to answer.

I am deeply grateful to the board of trustees of McCormick Theological Seminary for giving me leave from the president's office for the fall semester of 2003 and to the Ecumenical Institute at St. John's Abbey and University for accepting me as an ecumenical fellow and providing a wonderful setting for research and reflection. I am also grateful for opportunities to share this work in progress through various lectureships at the Presbytery of the Cascades; Madison Square Presbyterian Church, San Antonio; McCormick Theological Seminary; Austin Presbyterian Theological Seminary; and Austin College. Finally, I have been blessed during the writing, revising, and editing of this book by the support and fabulous cooking of my husband, Fred Holper.

1
Is This "My Father's" World or Not?

Religious diversity in the United States is not new news. In fact, it is as old as the country itself and was a significant issue in its founding. While we don't often think about it, the colonies of North America were made up of diverse religious groups who considered one another to be "other religions" rather than divergent streams of Christianity. The Christian diversity of the seventeenth and eighteenth centuries—Calvinists (both Presbyterian and Congregational), Anglicans, Baptists, Quakers, Lutherans, and Catholics—was not a matter of denominational variety, to use the analogy of currency. Many of these groups regularly referred to others as "heretics" or "apostate," rather than as members of the one body of Christ as we think of them today. Confessional variations at that time also reflected differences involving social separation and political persecution. The memory of warfare, imprisonment, and persecution based on religious differences was vivid for the founders of this nation, and political discrimination by one religious group against another was not unknown in the colonies themselves. As has often been argued, a government free from religious control and a nation that guaranteed freedom of religious practice were radical ideas in the eighteenth century. This distinctive form of government set the stage for even greater religious diversity in the United States in the twenty-first century.

Religious diversity in America is much greater today than at the nation's founding. Large cities like Chicago are home to faith communities representing all of the world's major religions, but even smaller communities are home to wide varieties of Christian groups, as well as Mormons, Muslims, Buddhists, Hindus, and Jews. We have become accustomed as a nation to seeing leaders of various "faith communities" represented in public ceremonies. Indeed, the presence of priests and pastors, imams and rabbis and monks, at prayer services such as those held after 9/11 was critical to reaffirming national unity.

My purpose in this book is not to explore or document religious diversity in American culture. That has already been done.[1] My purpose here is to engage in a conversation about how Christians might think about the phenomenon of religious diversity from a theological point of view that includes rather than excludes such diversity. Many Christians assume that affirmation of faith in Jesus Christ as Savior and Lord requires the rejection of all other religious traditions. In this chapter, I will explore that position but argue that it both presents serious theological problems for Christian faith and has negative consequences for living in a religiously diverse society. In the remaining chapters, I will attempt to show how it is possible to affirm the Christian confession that God has made Godself uniquely known to humankind in the life, death, and resurrection of Jesus and at the same time to affirm that the religious diversity of human history is part of God's providential care for all of humankind.

I am writing for Christians and for those wishing to see how Christians might understand these issues. I am not attempting to propose how those of other faith traditions should understand religious diversity. In fact, because religious traditions really are diverse, how religious diversity is an issue—and even whether it *is* an issue—depends on the nature of the tradition itself. The purpose of this work is to discuss the issue on Christian terms, in dialogue with Christian theology and the Bible. I will also not attempt to present a complete survey of the variety of Christian responses to religious diversity in the two thousand years of Christian history, as that has been done effectively by others.[2] My purpose is rather to make a theological argument that affirms the Christian confession, in both faith and practice, while also affirming the reality of religious diversity. One of the practical effects of this will be an increased ability for Christians to welcome and live in peace with the religious "others."

I have set out on this journey because many Christians would like to be able to affirm the faith of their tradition and their personal experience of Jesus as Savior and Lord while at the same time finding room for living with respect for the faith of neighbors, coworkers, and family members. For Christians, this is both a theological and a practical problem. The practical dimensions are obvious. In the past three or four decades, the issue of Christian relations with non-Christians has changed from being an abstract issue about people far away to a close-to-home issue involving people we see on a day-to-day basis. As recently as the 1960s, we could speak about the religious life of America falling within the "Judeo-Christian tradition." In fact, this phrase was brought into common usage as a way to create an umbrella of unity to cover the religious diversity that had finally been recognized in the America of "Protestant-Catholic-Jew."

THE NEW DIVERSITY

In 1965, a substantial revision of the immigration laws opened the United States to more persons coming from the nations of Asia and Africa. As a result, forty years later researchers estimate that there are more Muslims in the United States than there are Jews, Presbyterians, or Episcopalians, and more varieties of Buddhists in greater Los Angeles than any place else on earth. Large Hindu temples are being dedicated in major metropolitan areas, and mosques are being built in suburbia. Some fifteen years ago, as a pastor in central Kansas, I received a call one day from a funeral director in town asking what I knew about Buddhist funeral practices. The patriarch of the Cambodian community in town had died, and the family had come to my friend, who realized that he had no idea how to begin to help them.

Religious diversity has led to problems, however, in both private and public arenas. In some places requests from Islamic groups for building permits have been denied, leading to lawsuits alleging religious discrimination. Sikh men and Muslim women have reported difficulties in job interviews or at work when wearing traditional head coverings. Perhaps most troubling, some Christian groups have sought by various means to have the United States identify itself officially as a "Christian nation." After complaints from current and former students, an investigation was launched at the United States Air Force Academy in 2005 to determine whether Christian proselytizing was taking place in classrooms and other venues.

Most Christians, I believe, do not want to impose Christianity on their neighbors. They want to find ways to live together with others in ways that honor both their Christian instincts of extending hospitality to strangers and their American commitments to being "a nation of immigrants," one nation made up of people from many cultures.

Indeed, Christians often find that engagement with those from other religious traditions has helped them understand aspects of their own faith traditions and practices in new and deeper ways. Some ten years ago, a vice president of a major bank in Dallas told me about being named to a task force to sort out how to accommodate religious holidays for bank employees. He was one of two Christians, he said, in a group that included Jews, Muslims, Buddhists, Hindus, and Sikhs. Whereas official holidays for the bank and the financial markets basically included Christian observances such as Christmas, how could the bank find a way for those of other religious traditions to have time off for what are for them equally significant days to be in worship or with family? What helped him understand the importance that specific days for religious observance held for these others was a class he and his family had participated in at their church on the meaning of Advent and how to celebrate that season of the church year, as opposed to focusing on the commercial Christmas that has become common in our culture. The task force successfully revised the bank's personnel policies to accommodate time off for people of various religious traditions. In the process, the participants learned a deeper appreciation of the many ways people respond to God's presence in their daily lives.

For many other Christians, religious diversity is experienced much closer to home—in fact, in the home. Prior to World War II, a Protestant-Catholic wedding was considered an "interfaith" marriage. Thirty years ago, a Christian-Jewish wedding required significant negotiation. Today, pastors and families are learning how to blend worship services and family life between Christians and persons from many more religious traditions.

As is often the case, experience leads to rethinking theological affirmations. Many prominent Christian thinkers who have sought to develop a new Christian approach to religious diversity have themselves been missionaries or teachers in predominantly non-Christian nations. While in no way diminishing their commitment to Christ, these theologians have come to a profound respect for other religious traditions and for the ethical commitments that grow from them. Person-to-person experiences with those from other religious traditions and a recognition of the reality of the religiously diverse world we live in have opened the door to a new exploration of the issue. For Christians, however, religious diversity is a theological issue that must be explored theologically.

THE "THEOLOGICAL" PROBLEM

What do I mean that this is a "theological" issue? Religious traditions have different approaches to what practices constitute the core of that tradition. It is easy to see this even within Christianity. Some Christians worship in what are called "liturgical" traditions that follow written prayer books and prescribed ceremonies. Others leave the ordering of worship to a particular community and its own leaders. The ordering of Christian community varies from hierarchical churches to completely autonomous congregations. From an ecumenical perspective, these variations constitute the gifts that each tradition brings to the church as a whole.

One of the things that Christians share, although in varying degrees of formality, is the practice of "doing theology." In many ways, this is one of the distinctive marks of Christianity. I use the term theology in two ways here. First, Christian faith is centered on God, an orienting perspective we share with the other two "Abrahamic faiths," Judaism and Islam; all questions, wherever they start, always come back to our understanding of God. The nature of the human condition, ethical choices, ways of understanding authority (religious and otherwise): these are all theological questions, which is to say they are ultimately questions about the nature and purposes of God. Christianity, Judaism, and Islam also believe that humanity is created in the image and likeness of God; therefore all the issues that concern human life are rooted in one's understanding of the divine life. Or, as Reformed theologian John Calvin put it, knowledge of God and knowledge of self (humanity) are interdependent questions, two sides of the same coin. To say that a Christian approach to religious diversity is a "theological problem" means that it has to do with who we understand God to be and how we think God relates to the world.

A second meaning of "theological" gives further shape to this discussion. Theology is not only talk about God; it is the discipline of thinking and speaking about God in an orderly fashion. It is to think and speak within the boundaries of some broadly agreed-upon norms or rules. Here we see the distinctions among the broad confessional traditions within Christianity. Among Protestant Christians, talk about God will most often be closely tied to Scripture, and the Bible will most often be cited as the central authority when making a theological argument. Protestants will then bring in other sources and norms, such as experience (personal as well as cultural, intellectual, scientific, and artistic), reason, and religious tradition (the teaching of the church from the past). Catholic and Orthodox theologians will use roughly the same set of sources but may weight them differently, emphasizing the teaching authority of the church, the role of church councils and formal statements of dogma, or the teachings of particular theologians (like Gregory of Nyssa or Thomas Aquinas) whose work has shaped the tradition.

Until the last quarter of the twentieth century, Catholic and Protestant theology was almost exclusively the province of white men trained and, for the most part, teaching in the great universities of Europe and North America. The past thirty years have seen an explosion in the range of theological writing and of those participating in theological scholarship. Theologians from Latin America, although trained in Europe, began writing in conversation with political and social realities in their countries in the late 1960s and early 1970s. Women from across the world raised questions about the ways in which the voices and experience of women need to be heard in Christian thought, and women now contribute significantly to theology, biblical studies, and related areas. African American scholars have had significant impact not only in the United States but on theologians from Africa, India, and Asia. Most recently, theologians and church leaders from Asia (from India to Korea) have begun to publish their reflections on Christian faith from their context.

A unifying theme of these theological voices is the importance of context or "social location" for experiencing God and approaching Christian faith. The claim they make is that the situation of the interpreter shapes the way in which that interpreter reads the Bible and understands Christian tradition. This is true, they argue, not only for contemporary theologians but for the biblical writers and for all who have attempted to reflect on Christian experience. As a result, the work of theology has come to be seen less as the task of expressing "timeless truth" and more as discerning aspects of the truth of God as humans experience it in their particular personal and social contexts. While I as an individual or member of a faith community may not share the experience of the one reflecting and writing from a different context, their reflection may well shed light on the truth of God in ways that my own experience obscures or makes less obvious. Taken together, this variety of theological reflection has the potential to lead us all into an understanding of God that no one person or no one tradition can achieve alone.

This development in understanding the work of theology is particularly important for the question that I consider in this book. How as a Christian you deal with religious diversity depends on where you find yourself with respect to persons of different religious traditions. If non-Christians are people in "far away lands" (as they were for European and American Christians who mounted the modern missionary movements), then it is easy to see how Christians could claim they possessed the "truth of God" that they were bound to share with all others who did not know this truth. If, however, you are a Christian in a society and culture dominated by other long-standing and deeply held religious traditions, the question may begin to look somewhat different. In particular, one might well reflect differently on the question of where God has been with the people of this culture through all the generations of their life before Christian missionaries arrived. If you live, as Americans do now, in a nation with both deep Christian roots and a commitment to the free exercise of religion, how Christians relate to our many non-Christian neighbors, coworkers, and family members will be shaped precisely by this new reality.

The argument I have attempted to make thus far is that the question of how Christians understand and relate to religious diversity is a theological issue, a question of who we understand God to be and what we think God is up to in the world. Further, we will approach the question theologically, that is, in light of what we read in the Bible and how the church has reflected on the reading of Scripture through the ages. Finally, we will face this issue aware that we are Christian citizens of a newly religiously diverse nation.

How difficult this issue is to discuss can be illustrated by a recent experience of the Presbyterian Church. At a national conference on peacemaking in 2000, a Presbyterian minister who serves as executive director of the Council for the Parliament of the World's Religions made a statement in which he seemed to relativize the role of Jesus as Savior and Lord. After positively discussing the ethical commitments to peace and respect for life that Christians share with other religious traditions, he asked, "What's the big deal about Jesus?" Although the question was clearly rhetorical and he went on to answer it, that question was lifted out of context and a hue and cry raised for the speaker to be disciplined and for top denominational officials to reaffirm their confession that Jesus Christ is the only (or "unique") Savior of the whole world. The denominational office on theology and worship prepared a study document "Hope in the Lord Jesus Christ" that was affirmed by the General Assembly in 2001, but suspicion has remained, as has pressure for "doctrinal correctness" from more conservative parts of the church.

A similar incident in the Roman Catholic Church gained much broader attention. In 2000, the Congregation for the Doctrine of the Faith, headed by Joseph Cardinal Ratzinger (now Pope Benedict XVI) issued the Declaration "'Dominus Jesus' on the Unicity and Salvific Universality of Jesus Christ and the Church." As the title indicates, the purpose was to reinforce traditional teaching that Jesus Christ is the one and only Savior of the entire world and that the Roman Catholic Church is the only true expression of faith in Christ. After decades in which the Catholic Church expanded its relationships with other Christians and worked to establish dialogue between Catholics and Jews and Muslims, the document set off great anxiety, especially among theological scholars in the United States. One of the precipitating causes for the issuance of the declaration was the 1997 publication and subsequent investigation by the church of a magisterial work on religious diversity, *Toward a Christian Theology of Religious Pluralism*, by Jacques Dupuis, SJ. Dupuis's is a work of great depth and sophistication, based on his experience of teaching Christian theology for more than thirty-five years in India. While the Vatican has not withdrawn the statement, the public outcry about it has led the Vatican to take numerous measures to reiterate its commitment to Christian ecumenical relations and to affirm the importance of positive relations between Catholic Christians and Jews and Muslims. Indeed, soon after his election, Pope Benedict took steps to reaffirm the Catholic Church's commitments to both ecumenical and interfaith relations.

Religious diversity is increasingly important in today's world. How Christians approach the issue has serious political and social as well as theological implications. For some time, the conversation among those writing about this matter has suggested that the various Christian approaches can be seen as ranging along a continuum. Three major positions are identified as "exclusivism," "inclusivism," and "pluralism."[3] I will look at these briefly and attempt to show why each position fails to provide an adequate account of how Christians understand our own faith tradition as well as the traditions of others.

EXCLUSIVISM

The best place to begin this discussion is with what might be called the "traditional" Christian position with respect to religious diversity. This view, sometimes termed "exclusivism," in other circles is simply known as Christian orthodoxy. Christian faith was born out of Judaism and grew up in the Mediterranean world of religious diversity. In that context of controversy and the struggle for self-definition and differentiation, Christian Scriptures appear to present a fairly clear response to the issue of religious diversity. Indeed, for some Christians today, certain New Testament texts seem to stand out in boldface print. John 14:6: "I am the way, the truth, and the life. No one comes to the Father except through me." Acts 4:12: "There is salvation in no one else [than Jesus], for there is no other name under heaven given among mortals by which we must be saved." Philippians 2:10–11: "At the name of Jesus every knee should bend, in heaven and on earth and under the earth, and every tongue should confess that Jesus Christ is Lord, to the glory of God the Father."

These texts, coupled with the "great commission" of Matthew 28:19 ("Go therefore and make disciples of all nations . . ."), seem to set the agenda for Christian mission. Jesus is the one and only way to God and to salvation, and it is the task of Christians to bring this saving faith to all people. A slightly softer way to state this position is to say that faith in Jesus Christ is the only way to God and eventually (that is, in the eschaton or at the end of time) all people will have the opportunity to recognize the Lordship of Christ and come to saving faith. But the end result is the same: the only way to a saving relationship with God is through faith in Jesus Christ. All others will end up outside the grace of God.

Why is this view problematic? For some Christians past and present, this view is not problematic at all. Citing verses that suggest that Christ died for "the righteous," these Christians argue that the effects of the saving death of Christ are not intended to apply to the whole of humanity, but only to those who make profession of faith or who have been elected (specifically chosen) by God to receive the benefits of salvation. This view, sometimes called "limited atonement," was widely taught by Dutch and English Calvinists and has had a significant impact on American evangelical thought. Another way of expressing a similar notion comes from the pre-Reformation tradition that "outside the church there is no salvation." In this view, the path to salvation is only through Christ, and the way to Christ is through participation in the sacramental life of the church.

Because one can make a scriptural case for both of these versions of "Christian exclusivism," why would one call such a theological view into question? The most straightforward answer is that it seems at odds with other things we believe about God and at the same time makes it difficult to live with neighbors who are not Christian.

If there is reason to question Christian exclusivism, how might this be done? One might make an argument for or against any theological point of view in a number of ways. One question to ask is whether the view is true to Scripture. In this case, the question is whether exclusivism is true to the full sweep of Scripture, not just to isolated verses read in a certain way. This, in fact, is the issue I will pursue in the following chapters.

Another question to be asked in examining a particular theological perspective is an ethical question: What are the practical consequences of holding such a point of view? This takes Jesus' statement that "by their fruits you will know them" and applies it to Christian doctrine. That is, what are, or have been, the consequences of believing in a certain way? While the answer cannot be proven definitively, it is true historically that when Christian exclusivism has been reinforced by political and military power, the results have often been devastating. For centuries, Christian Europe demonized, marginalized, and persecuted Jews in ways that provided a foundation for the extermination attempted by the Nazis. The Crusades of the Middle Ages and attempts to "liberate" the Holy Land from the "infidel" were wars fueled by the ideology of Christian exclusivism. These efforts culminated in the expulsion of Jews and Muslims from Spain in 1492 and in the Inquisition that followed, during which Jews who remained were given the option of conversion or execution. After the Reformation, Christian exclusivism became an internal battle in which national armies became involved in struggles for which the "true church" was defending the "true faith." Not all who espouse Christian exclusivism have used violence or coercive power. But the fact is that this doctrine, when coupled with political power, has led to actions that are clearly at odds with other aspects of Christian faith. This should cause us to raise at least some questions about the validity of the idea.

Yet another question to be asked about any particular theological idea is, How does it fit with other ideas that the tradition affirms? This is a question of coherence or consistency. In this respect, Christian exclusivism raises a number of questions that it has difficulty answering effectively. First of all, if salvation comes only to those who profess faith in Jesus Christ, what about all the people who lived before Christ and never had the opportunity to hear about him? Orthodox or traditional Christian doctrine has taught that (for reasons seemingly known only in the providence of God) this vast segment of humankind is simply condemned to live and die outside the gracious promise of God.

In the Reformed tradition, this position is stated explicitly in the Westminster Larger Catechism: "Question 60: Can they who have never head the gospel, and so know not Jesus Christ nor believe in him, be saved by their living according to the light of nature? Answer: They who having never heard the gospel, know not Jesus Christ, and believe not in him, cannot be saved, be they never so diligent to frame their lives according to the laws of nature, or the laws of that religion which they profess."[4] But this leads to the obvious question, Why would a God in whose image all people were created, a God the Bible says loves all of creation, devise a plan of salvation that would automatically exclude most of the humans who have ever lived? Put another way, how does this view of Christian exclusivism (and in this case limited salvation) square with other things Christians believe about the goodness of God and God's care for all creation?

INCLUSIVISM

A number of biblical passages suggest that an approach other than the exclusivist is warranted. Obviously, the Psalms and the later prophets all bear witness to the idea that God is Lord of all nations and all creation, that all the earth is full of the glory of God, that all peoples serve God and God's purposes. Isaiah's vision of the "end times" is that "all nations" will come to the mountain of the Lord (to Zion) and live in peace. Paul echoes this vision when he proclaims that "in Christ God was reconciling the world to himself" (2 Cor. 5:19) or "reconcil[ing] to himself all things, whether on earth or in heaven" (Col. 1:20).

As to the question of who will be saved, John 10:16 suggests a broader rather than more narrow view: "I have other sheep that do not belong to this fold."

Several theological approaches have been suggested recently that build on this biblical vision. The first (both chronologically and in order of impact) comes from the Roman Catholic tradition. Two documents from the Second Vatican Council in the 1960s (*Lumen Gentium* or "The Dogmatic Constitution on the Church" and *Nostra Aetate* or "The Declaration on the Relation of the Church to Non-Christian Religions") broke new theological ground by asserting that Christians can expect God to work in saving ways in the hearts of those who have never heard the gospel but who seek to follow the guidance of conscience. This view builds on traditional Catholic teaching that, despite the effects of sin, human beings are able to respond to God's presence, to know good from evil, and seek to do what pleases God. *Nostra Aetate* in particular acknowledges positive aspects (what it calls the "spiritual and moral truths") of non-Christian religions and encourages Christians to engage in both dialogue and "collaboration" with others.[5] These truths are only a part, however, of the fullness of truth that is revealed by God in Jesus Christ, who is the one in whom all humanity will eventually be reconciled and reunited. Religious diversity is, in the last analysis, a temporary rather than permanent feature of human life.

A very similar approach has been expressed recently in evangelical circles by Canadian theologian Clark Pinnock, who argues that the "particularity" of the Christian claim that salvation is through Jesus Christ alone must always be held in tension with another, equally important truth, namely, the "universality" of God's love for all creation and all persons. The most important thing Christians know about God because of Christ is that God is gracious and generous. While not willing to grant that other religions can be "ordinary means" of salvation, Pinnock argues forcefully that we must presume God's presence to all and God's ability to use other religious paths in God's ultimate plan of redemption and reconciliation.[6]

Finally, Presbyterian theologian George Hunsinger has explored a position he calls "generous orthodoxy." He begins with the premise that however salvation happens, it finally depends on the gracious act of God. This builds on the Reformed understanding of the doctrine of election which states that salvation is the result of God's free choice or grace. It is not our faith that saves us, because faith itself is possible only because of God's presence and activity in our lives. Thus, the entire question of salvation rests with God and not with us. We do not seek God; we are sought and found. And we are not the ones to judge who will be saved and who will not. Whatever limits there may be to salvation, they are known only to God. To the question of what will happen to those who follow other religious traditions, Hunsinger writes, "God has made salvation available to all human beings through Jesus Christ, crucified and risen. How God will deal with those who do not know or follow Christ, but who follow another tradition, we cannot finally say. We can say, however, that God is gracious and merciful, and that God will not deal with people in any other way than we see in Jesus Christ, who came as the savior of the world."[7]

These three positions, coming from Catholic, evangelical, and mainline Protestant branches of the Christian faith, might broadly be called "inclusivist" in their approach. For all the important distinctions that can be noted among them, these positions share two important ideas. First, the issue at stake is the distinctive question posed by Christian faith, namely, who will be saved and how? Christian faith is built around the view that God and humankind are estranged as a result of human sin and that God sets this right by means of the life, death, and resurrection of Jesus Christ. In Paul's terms, in Christ, God is reconciling the world to Godself. As many have pointed out, however, this is not the only religious question there is, nor is it the question that all religions or religious people in fact ask. A fuller discussion of this idea follows in chapter 4.

The second thing that these three variations of Christian inclusivism have in common is their desire to hold in tension two different theological ideas. In Pinnock's terms, these are the universality of God's care for all and the particularity of God's revelation in Jesus Christ. Each in a different way, these approaches suggest that in the end whatever religious diversity has existed in the history of humankind will fall away, when all are finally reconciled by God through Jesus Christ. These theologies are essentially optimistic: in the end, God's grace will win out, and all creation will be transformed and renewed. If some are eternally "lost," it will be a finite number who have turned away from God, and in any case the question finally rests with a God whose mercy "endures forever." This confidence in the scope of God's mercy makes these views "inclusive" with respect to the paradigm of approaches to religious diversity. Eventually all diversity will be gathered up or included in God's love for the world in Jesus Christ.

Generous as this approach seems, critics say that inclusivism is simply exclusivism with a kinder, gentler face. In the end, it amounts to the same thing: there is only one way to salvation or right relationship with God, and that is the Christian way. Put another way, the purposes and activity of God for all people who have ever lived are finally defined by what Christians believe God was and is doing in Jesus Christ. However kindly one might put it, this means that the other religions have at best partial truth and are finally simply wrong with respect to their view of reality. Even granting that those who follow these other traditions may yet be found by the mercy of God, these people have been deluded during their lifetime and will only come to the full truth at the end of time. Is not such a view condescending to others? And does such a view claim too much knowledge of God, knowledge which all Christians affirm humans will never have completely?

PLURALISM

For these and other reasons, a third approach to the issue of religious diversity has arisen. In the terms of the paradigm we have been using, it is called "pluralism." First, a word of caution about terminology. In some discussions, the words "diversity" and "pluralism" are used almost interchangeably, but it is important to distinguish between them. I use "diversity" here as a descriptive term: it is simply the fact that there is among human beings a wide variety of religious traditions and practices. I use "pluralism," by contrast, to describe an approach to this fact of religious diversity. This approach argues that there is no one right way to be religious, that the religions of the world's peoples each have their own integrity, and that every attempt should be made to understand and respect the various religions on their own terms.

Some argue that this is the position implicitly taken by the U.S. Bill of Rights: All religions are to be equally respected because all are protected under the "free exercise" clause. Often the approach is voiced in popular culture. We hear people say that whatever religion a person professes, it is a private matter, something between that person and "his or her God." In some discussions about spirituality, people will say something like, "There are many paths, but we are all climbing the same mountain."

However, this form of laissez-faire relativism is critiqued by almost everyone who thinks and writes seriously about the issues of religious diversity. Religions make claims about the nature of reality, and they embody values and urge ethical practices that have real consequences when lived out in community. To gloss over these differences is not only disrespectful; in some cases, it is dangerous. To pretend that religious differences don't make a difference in the way people live, both in private and in public, is simply naive.

Most who argue in favor of pluralism as an approach to religious diversity do not fall into these obvious traps. They do, however, make the argument that the various religions are specific ways of pointing towards a larger reality that stands behind them. Philosopher John Hick has been a strong exponent of this position. Specific religious doctrines or worldviews are, he argues, human attempts to respond to ultimate reality. The experience of the transcendent is by definition beyond any human attempt to understand or express it. The religions of humanity are means by which different cultures and people have sought to be in relationship with the divine reality that is ultimately beyond the grasp of any. Hick's view is indeed similar to the notion of "many paths," but standing behind it is a philosophic argument about the nature of reality that supports the possibility of multiple religious expressions.

Pluralism of this kind has also been widely criticized. Obviously, it is rejected by those who hold to the view that their own religious tradition (Christian or otherwise) is based on God's specific self-disclosure and is the sole truth about reality and matters like salvation. It is also severely criticized by those who advocate a more open approach on the basis of interfaith dialogue. The problem with Hick's view, they suggest, is that he in fact is willing to gloss over the real religious differences that exist, differences that must be taken into account if religious people are going to talk and work and live together. Intellectually, the problem is that, in order to make his argument work, Hick has to posit a reality ("God beyond God," as it is sometimes called) that has no place in any of the religions as actually practiced. Others argue that the approach he suggests is reductionist. Hick makes a critical mistake by collapsing the "ends" or religious goals of the various religions into something that looks much like what Christians call "salvation," a concept that has no exact parallel in other traditions.[8]

WHERE DO WE GO FROM HERE?

We have looked briefly at three general approaches to the phenomenon of religious diversity. The purpose of this project is to explore whether these are the only options for faithful Christians. Each of the approaches has significant challenges. Exclusivism, in my judgment, fails to account for the full range of the biblical tradition and for the "wideness of God's mercy." Inclusivism, for all its breadth of view, often ends up being exclusivism more politely stated. Pluralism, at least as most often stated, fails because it glosses over the real religious differences and ends up in a relativism that fails to take religious commitment seriously. Are these the only options for faithful Christians? Is there another way to approach the issue? In particular, the question I wish to pose is this: Is it possible for Christians to understand the great variety of religious traditions and practices as part of God's providential plan for humankind? Is it possible that to affirm that God seeks and is found by human beings through the many religious "ways" that have been and are followed, and still affirm the saving grace of God in Jesus Christ?

Three core values or commitments lead me to explore these hypotheses and guide this book. First, peace is to be valued above conflict, violence, and warfare. All religion should "seek peace and pursue it." Thus, I evaluate theological approaches to religious diversity in terms of whether and how they contribute to peace. Second, Christians should respect and attempt to understand the religions of others on their own terms, as a matter of Christian hospitality or welcoming of the stranger. I believe that this great Christian virtue should shape not only our behavior, but also our thinking about religious diversity. Third, religious and philosophical differences do make a difference; beliefs matter. Any discussion of religious diversity must deal with questions of truth. The notion that "it doesn't matter what you believe as long as you are sincere" makes a mockery of *all* religious traditions, including the Christian.

With these convictions, we turn to a review of some biblical and theological themes that may suggest a way to think about the phenomenon of religious diversity.

2

Many Faiths—One Family

The Bible is not a book of theology in the sense of being a logical or orderly reflection on the nature of God. No where does the Bible set out to "prove" the existence of God. God is simply assumed. In fact, the Bible is primarily a narrative in which the first and most important character is God. The Bible is the story of God and God's relationship to humanity. In particular, it is the story of God's relationship (in the Old Testament) with Israel and (in the New) with the followers of Jesus, who come to be known as the body of Christ or the church. While these two "communities" are the primary focus of God's relationship, it is clear in both testaments that these specific relationships have implications for the way we are to understand God's relationship to all creation and all peoples. In this chapter, we will examine the way in which the Old Testament looks at the question of other religions and the status of those who follow them. In the next chapter, we will consider the role of the religious "others" in the story of Jesus. Examination of these narratives will guide our thinking about how we might think theologically about the diversity of religious life in our world today.

The Old Testament is well aware that there are "other" peoples, nations, cultures, and religions in the world. Whether or not there are other "gods" is a question that seems to show some evolution of understanding. In some places, Yahweh is spoken of as being "above all other gods." The first statement in the Ten Commandments is: "You shall have no other gods before (or besides) me" (Exod. 20:3), which might be read to suggest that there were thought to be "other gods" that are simply of lesser status. Elsewhere, however, the assertion is made that there is only one God and that the gods of the other nations are merely "idols" (Ps. 96:5).

When we ask how the Bible understands the variety of religions, we find a similarly varied set of responses. According to the dominant view, there is only one God and there is only one "chosen people" among all others. The vocation of this people is to become a "holy nation" loyal to God alone. After the exodus, this task meant settling in the "promised" land of Canaan, defeating the people already settled there, and creating a nation. In the narratives of Joshua and Judges, the "others" are clearly enemies to be defeated and sometimes destroyed.

Later, during the stories of the monarchies, the religions of the other peoples of the region are portrayed as temptations to Israel to forsake God and worship "idols." Idolatry is an issue for Israel in two related but distinctively different ways. The first issue is the Old Testament view that the worship of other gods is simply wrongheaded, because these are not even remotely divine; they are "false" gods because they are not "gods" at all. As Psalm 115 puts it, the idols are things made by human hands; they have no life in them. And "those who make them are like them" (v. 8). Worship of idols leads to death. The second fundamental issue is that Israel has promised to be loyal to Yahweh alone, as Yahweh has promised loyalty to Israel. The covenant renewal story at the end of Joshua (see chapters 23 and 24) is representative of this theme of reciprocal allegiance between God and Israel. One important theme then of the Old Testament narrative is that there is true religion and false; to worship anything other than the God of Israel is idolatry; to worship any other god is to be unfaithful or disloyal to the God of the covenant.

It would be tempting to conclude that the view of the Old Testament with respect to other religions and those who follow them is simply and completely "exclusive," to use the terms discussed in the previous chapter. While it is possible to read the Old Testament and focus only on the story line that emphasizes that God is "a jealous God," both a larger story line and an intriguing set of characters and narratives run counter to the narrative of exclusivism.

REREADING GENESIS

The larger story line begins at the beginning and can be seen clearly in Genesis 1–11. In the canonical ordering of Scripture, the story of God and humankind begins with the creation of the first humans. In the first version of that story, we read that humans are made in the "image and likeness" of God. The charge God gives to human beings is that they "be fruitful and multiply, and fill the earth and subdue it" (Gen. 1:28). Thus begins the human story. From these few verses, we see, first of all, that all humankind shares a common origin; all can trace their origins to these first ones created in the divine image. Second, we see that God has a vision for the human family, namely, that they spread out across the earth, multiply, and "subdue" or domesticate the land. As the narrative unfolds, that is precisely what happens. But something else happens as well: "the wickedness of humankind was great in the earth." (Gen. 6:5) Over these ten (very long) generations from the "first parents," humanity has multiplied numerically, but it has also increased the evil in the world. The result, according to the story, is that God is "sorry" that God created humankind in the first place and vows to wipe them out.

One man, however, is found to be righteous. Noah, described as a "righteous" man who "walked with God" (6:9), is charged with the task of building an ark that will serve as a refuge during the destructive flood that is to follow. Noah and his family and the pairs of animals that Noah brings into the ark will be the source for regenerating or renewing the creation. After the flood subsides and the land dries out, Noah and his family and the animals emerge from the ark. God repeats the command given to the first human beings: "Be fruitful and multiply, and fill the earth" (9:1). Then God makes a covenant with Noah, with all Noah's descendants, and "with every living creature that is with you" (9:10). This universal covenant might be called the "covenant of life." God promises never again to destroy life on earth (9:8–17). God also prohibits the taking of human life. There is an explicit link back to the beginning: the shedding of human blood is forbidden, because all are created in the image of God (9:6).

Notice that this covenant is not particular to Israel. This promise precedes the selection of one group to be "God's own people" and is for all creation and all humanity, for all time. In the biblical view, then, there was a universal covenant before there was a particular relationship with Israel. In recent years, this theme has become important in Jewish thinking, especially as it provides common ground for Jewish-Christian dialogue. Jewish theologian Irving Greenberg, for example, sees the covenant with Noah as setting forth a relationship between Creator and creation based on love and the preservation of life. Thus he concludes that "every religion that works to repair the world—and thus advance the triumph of life—is a valid expression of this divine pact with humanity."[1]

As with all the other covenants that will follow, this relationship is initiated entirely by God. God creates the world and human beings at God's own initiative. God then enters into relationship with humankind from God's free initiative. In this story, God also binds Godself, placing a limit on God's own freedom for the sake of the life of creation and humankind. Everything else that follows in the biblical tradition with respect to particular covenants or God's "exclusive" relationship, either with Israel or with Christians, needs to be read in light of this fundamental covenant of life.

What happens after this familiar story is an important turning point in the narrative of Genesis. The charge God gives to Noah and his family is to return to the original design, that is, to repopulate the earth. The implication is that they are to spread out, to settle in different places, and to create human civilization. In Genesis 10 we find a set of genealogies of Noah's sons, Japheth, Ham, and Shem. Each of these sets of descendants is described as having their own lands or territory and languages.

These genealogies are interrupted in Genesis 11:1–9 by a story that seems to have been intentionally placed there. I say intentionally because it begins with the words, "Now the whole earth had one language and the same words." At some time prior to the division of the families and languages, the story says that these descendants of Noah have been traveling "from the east" and decide to settle down on the plain of Shinar. There they decide to build a city and a tower. They want to give up their nomadic life and build a community. They want to stay together as an extended family; they do not want to be separated or scattered across the face of the earth. As the text says, they want to "make a name for themselves." That is, they want to be remembered by future generations and to be thought well of.

The traditional reading of what happens next is often called the "pride and punishment" interpretation.[2] God comes down to see this city that the people have begun to build. The project appears to be surprising to God; this is not part of the plan, which was for these people to disperse and populate the whole earth. God describes the problem as follows: "They are one people and they have all one language." God's solution is to "confuse their language" (11:7) so that they will no longer be able to understand one another and then to scatter the people across the face of the earth.

According to the traditional interpretation, the act of building focuses on the tower rather than the city (in fact, the story is popularly known as "the tower of Babel"). The tower is often interpreted as an assault on heaven, on God's personal space. To build a tower such as this is thought to be an act of hubris or overbearing pride on the part of humanity. God is jealous or angry or both, and rebuffs the disobedient humans by destroying their building, confusing their languages and scattering them across the world. Thus, the traditional interpretation suggests, the diversity of cultures and languages is a sign of God's punishment for the sin of human pride. The unity of humanity that the people tried to maintain by building the city is seen as a threat of some kind to God's power; the diversity that results and the difficulty of understanding one another are humanity's punishment.

On such a view, diversity is not only a challenge but sometimes an obstacle to communication and a source of friction and conflict. Diversity is a constant reminder that things are not as they should be, that we live in a broken and fearful world. This reading is reinforced for Christians when this story is read alongside Acts 2, the story of the first Pentecost. In that experience of the outpouring of the Holy Spirit, the gathered disciples become able to speak in other languages. In this powerful story, the damage done at Babel seems to have been repaired. The list of places in Acts 2:9–11 is almost a geography lesson of the places and cultures around the Mediterranean. The point is that people from all over the known world understand what a handful of Palestinian Jews are saying about Jesus. The destructive consequences of Babel are reversed by the "miracle of Pentecost."

A different reading of Genesis 11 is possible, however, one that suggests a different understanding of the origins and purposes of cultural (and, by extension, religious) diversity. Among the first to present this approach was one of the most noted Jewish interpreters of the Middle Ages, Ibn Ezra. Ezra pioneered a style of exegesis that favored a straightforward or grammatical reading of the text, in place of allegorical or mystical readings favored at the time. In terms that sound almost modern, Ezra argued that one should first of all read a text at face value rather than bringing to it already developed theological assumptions.

Following Ezra's suggestion, Old Testament scholar Theodore Hiebert argues that there is no *textual* reason to read this story as one of pride and punishment. Rather, this story can just as well be read as a text that explains the origin of the cultural and linguistic diversity enumerated in Genesis 10 in the context of God's original intention for creation. As Hiebert points out, the problem that God identifies when God comes to survey the construction of the city is *not* the building project or the tower per se. The problem from God's point of view is that the people have not *scattered*, but rather have chosen to stay together. Their desire for consolidation is made concrete by the fact that they all have one language. This unity achieved through uniformity and conformity takes the form of the construction of a city. The fact that cities in ancient times were walled adds to the picture of insularity. Recall that the charge to Noah and his children after the flood repeats God's charge to the first humans: be fruitful and multiply and fill the earth. This cannot be accomplished by staying together; scattering is necessary for the plan to be fulfilled.

It is true that God is displeased by the decision to build the city and the tower. But the problem is not the sin of pride, but the disobedience of God's command to scatter and fill the earth. God needs the scattering of humankind in order to fulfill God's plan for creation.

Among the several important steps in his argument, Hiebert points out that the traditional reading of the story is tied to a matter of translation. The critical word in Hebrew *blal* (from which the name "Babel" is derived) is usually translated "confused" or "confounded." As such, the negative implications are obvious. But in every other context in the Pentateuch where this word is used, it is translated as "mixed." In fact, the most common use of this verb is in the instructions given to priests about the proper ways to mix the ingredients used in offerings made to God. If *balal* means "mixed up" rather than "confused," then this story becomes a much more straightforward account of how things got to be the way they are (with respect to cultural and linguistic diversity), not an archetypal story about pride and punishment.

Another key to this reading is to shift the way we think about the subdivisions of the narrative in Genesis. If we think about the story of Noah and the covenant as the final event in the prehistory narrative, then the Babel story opens the section that deals with the "historical" characters. This is obvious in the canonical text, because after the story of Babel, the genealogy continues and ends with the father of Abram. On this reading, Babel is not the tragic end of the prehistory, but rather the opening scene in which humanity is put back on track to settle the earth. Then, from among the world's peoples God will choose Abraham and Sarah, through whom God promises to bless all the people of the earth. As Hiebert concludes, "Diversity is not the consequence of the sin of pride. . . . It is rather the outgrowth of God's own design for human culture. Such a theology views cultural diversity not as a lamentable condition which might have been avoided if humanity had only been good enough, but rather as the divine intention for the world which must be embraced."[3]

What does this reading suggest about the way we read Acts 2? If the diversity of languages and cultures is not a punishment for sin, but rather a fulfillment of the divine intention for humanity to spread out and fill the whole earth, then what is the "miracle of Pentecost" all about? Perhaps, in fact, this reading of Genesis 11 helps us understand Acts more accurately. The gift of "tongues" in Acts 2 is clearly not the "spiritual language" that Paul discusses in his letters. What happens at Pentecost is a kind of "simultaneous translations." The disciples are not speaking a heavenly language, a spiritual Esperanto, but rather multiple human languages. The miracle is that the audience hears each one "in the native language of each." The gift of the Spirit does not wipe out linguistic difference. Rather, the Spirit makes interlinguistic and cross-cultural communication possible. Pentecost sends the signal that, as we shall discuss in a later chapter, the promise of God is indeed for all peoples and nations, symbolized by the disciples' ability to use multiple languages.

In this section I have attempted to show that the Old Testament begins with a narrative of literally universal scope, culminating in God's covenant with all humanity. God has a plan for and cares about *all* of humankind. This story of God's intention for the whole human family is the context from which the particular stories of Israel and the Christian community emerge. But there are other parts of the Old Testament that have clues for how to understand cultural and/or religious diversity. In the next section, various characters and incidents are examined for what they may tell us about the place and purpose of such diversity in God's providence.

THE RELIGIOUS "OTHER" IN THE OLD TESTAMENT

Perhaps the most interesting way to answer questions about how the Old Testament understands religious diversity is to look for the places where religious outsiders or "others" appear in the story of Israel. Obviously many of the "others" are enemies, and much of the story of the contact between the other nations and Israel is about warfare, conquest, and violence. Even there, however, the lines are not hard and fast. Before Egypt was the oppressive empire from which Moses led the escape, Egypt was the refuge for Israel during times of famine. Indeed, the descendants of Abraham, Isaac, and Jacob settled in Egypt due to the leadership of Joseph in the pharaoh's government. Centuries later, when Israel is liberated from captivity in Babylon, the "liberator" is none other than Cyrus, the leader of what becomes the Persian dynasty. The clear view of the Bible is that these nations (like Israel itself) are subordinate to the larger plans of God. Through their own policies and actions, they serve God's purposes for Israel and thus demonstrate the working out of the relationship between God and Israel, which is ultimately for the "blessing" or redemption of the whole world. Even more interesting than the way the nation-states figure into the story of God and Israel is the way individual characters appear at various points in the story and play significant roles. They are and remain "Gentiles"; they are religious "others," and while they are not explicitly part of God's people, they receive God's blessing in various ways. It is especially intriguing to notice how many of the "others" are women.

The first such character is Hagar, Sarah's Egyptian slave (Gen. 16). When Sarah is unable to conceive an heir to fulfill the promise God has made to fill the earth with Abraham and Sarah's descendants, Sarah proposes that Abraham attempt to conceive a child with Hagar and thus produce an heir through what we might call a "surrogate" relationship. After Hagar gives birth to Ishmael, Sarah becomes pregnant and gives birth to Isaac, and God's "original" plan is back on track. The presence of Hagar and Ishmael is deeply upsetting to Sarah, and she appeals to Abraham to exile them to the wilderness. She asks him to send them out to die. When Abraham resists this cruel proposal, he is told by God that this child also will become the ancestor of a great nation "because he is your offspring" (21:13).

Out in the wilderness, the meager supply of bread and water runs out. Hagar sets the child down under a bush and withdraws, because she cannot bear to see the child die. But God hears the voice of the child and sends an angel to repeat the promise to Hagar that her son will live to give rise to a great nation. The angel leads Hagar to a well, she rescues Ishmael, and he grows up to become the father of the Arab peoples. According to the Qur'an, he is the ancestor of Muhammad whom Islam calls the "last of the prophets." In recent years, this idea that Jews, Muslims, and Christians share a common ancestor in Abraham has played a major role in interreligious dialogue, even to the extent of calling the three "Abrahamic faiths."

A number of other women who come from outside the people of Israel enter the story through marriage. Joseph, when he has become an official in the court of the pharaoh in Egypt, marries Asenath, daughter of an Egyptian priest. Their sons, Manasseh and Ephraim, become heads of two tribes of Israel (Gen. 41:50–52). Moses, although born to the tribe of Levi (later the priestly tribe), is raised in the household of the pharaoh. After he murders an Egyptian for assaulting a Hebrew, Moses escapes from Egypt and settles in Midian. There he marries Zipporah, daughter of a priest of Midian (Exod. 2).

Among these women from other cultures and religions whose story is best known is Ruth, the grandmother of David. According to this story, a man from Bethlehem in Judah took his wife and sons over to Moab (what is now Jordan) during a time of famine. After he died, the sons married Moabite women, one of whom was Ruth. In a well-known and beautifully told story of loyalty and devotion, Ruth leaves her family to accompany her mother-in-law Naomi back to Israel. There she and Naomi work out a plan to secure a marriage between Ruth and Boaz, a distant relative of Naomi's late husband, thereby providing for herself and Naomi. Though she comes from another culture and religious group, Ruth is incorporated into the family story of Israel to such an extent that she appears in the genealogy of Jesus in Matthew. Despite the various warnings against intermarriage, these women stand out as important figures in Israel's story.

In addition, it should be noted that although the story told in the book of Ruth is old, many scholars believe that it was written during the time of the events narrated in the books of Ezra and Nehemiah in the fifth century BCE. So this story may represent a reaction against the postexilic laws against intermarriage and the separation the other texts advocate from those of other cultural or religious traditions.[4]

Another group of Old Testament characters are often called "the righteous Gentiles" or "holy pagans." These characters appear both before and after the covenants and are regarded as worthy or approved by God, even though they do not know or follow the God of Israel. The book of Hebrews in the New Testament singles out some of them: Abel, whose offering was approved by God; Enoch, so righteous that he was taken up to heaven and escaped death; Noah, whose story we have already considered; and Melchizedek, priest of the "Most High God" who blesses Abraham and becomes the model for the priesthood of the Messiah.

The story of Job, one of these "righteous Gentiles," is presented at length. Job is set forth as a model of righteous man who remains faithful to God despite pain, suffering, and loss. The speeches of Job and his friends form an extended reflection on the classic problem of the relationship between a righteous life and the question of reward and punishment.

What is intriguing for our purposes is that at various points within the story of Israel, persons from outside the community come to have prominent roles. They are people who move the story forward, people upon whom the future of Israel depends. The message appears to be that purposes of God are big enough to include "others" who do not belong to Israel, because they still belong to God.

Perhaps the most intriguing story in the Old Testament that deals directly with the question of the status of those who follow other religions is the book of Jonah. This short story, probably from the postexilic period (sixth to fourth centuries BCE), is generally read as a parable illustrating how the mercy of God triumphs over God's justice. Jonah, a Jewish prophet, is charged to go to Nineveh, which is described as a great city, but is in fact the capital of the Assyrian Empire. His mission is to call the people, whom the text identifies as "very wicked," to repent. Jonah resists God's call and sets out by ship in the opposite direction. When a great storm arises, the sailors cast lots to determine who on board might have angered the gods. The lot falls to Jonah, who is thrown overboard and swallowed by the "great fish." Jonah prays to God for deliverance and is spewed out onto the shore.

The call from God comes once again, and Jonah sets out for Nineveh to deliver God's message of warning. Much to Jonah's amazement (and the reader's), the citizens repent, and God decides to spare them. Jonah is undone and complains bitterly about this egregious show of mercy: "This is why I fled to Tarshish at the beginning; for I knew that you are a gracious God and merciful" (Jonah 4:2). Jonah is so angry at God that he thinks it better to die, but God has the last word: "Should I not be concerned about [RSV: have pity on] Nineveh?" (4:11).

Commentators generally argue that this story is a morality tale rather than an attempt to narrate an event in Israel's history. Nineveh is generic for a big, corrupt city. But if corruption was the only point, the city could have been almost any place in Israel. The fact that Jonah is sent to the capital of an enemy empire cannot be accidental. The point is not a generic point that (on balance) God's mercy triumphs over God's justice. The point is that the mercy of God extends precisely to those who are thought to be outside the plan and beyond the pale. God sends Jonah to the people to whom Jonah doesn't want to go, but it is precisely those people ("and much cattle") who have occasioned God's mercy. It is a classic example of the mercy or love of God being broader than the measure of our human, even our religious, minds.

RELIGIOUS DIVERSITY IN THE HUMAN FAMILY

Before attempting do draw conclusions from this all too brief summary of the Old Testament, I want to repeat some of the foundational principles that guide this discussion about the topic of religious diversity. First, in chapter 1, I said that this is a *theological* question, as well as one that must be approached *theologically.* By "theological," I mean that the question of religious diversity is first a question about God. For Christians, and especially for Protestants from the Reformed family, every question comes back eventually to being a question about the nature and purposes of God. Second, and equally important, the question of how Christians are to understand the phenomenon of religious diversity must be approached *theologically.* Our task here is not to present various kinds of data about religions; and the question here is neither historical (how did various religious traditions arise and evolve?) nor sociological (what is the role of the religions in the development and maintenance of human society?). The task is rather to ask about the status of religious diversity in light of what our tradition, our sources, and our experience with God tell us.

The third thing to keep in mind is that we are asking this question in the only way we can, that is, as *Christians*. Other religious traditions have their own ways of accounting for, understanding, and relating to religious diversity. Indeed, most of the other major religions will have as much variation in their answers as Christianity does. This book is one Christian's attempt to account for and understand what the diversity of human religious life means for Christians. I have put the question this way because I think there are no other real alternatives. We can only ask questions such as this from the particular vantage points that we occupy. There is no "neutral ground" from which to ask about the relative status of different religious traditions. There is only the religious ground occupied by the one asking the question. Thus one's approach to the question will depend precisely upon the distinctive religious tradition that the questioner follows. How one accounts for and understands religious diversity is, therefore, a different issue for people of different traditions, that is, for Christians, Jews, Muslims, Hindus, Buddhists, and so on. There may be very good reason to compare those accounts and to look at one's own position in the light of those of others. In fact, the reflection of Jewish theologians will be instructive in this chapter in particular.

But the first task is to come to an understanding of the issue from within one's own religious tradition and practice. For this discussion, then, it is a *Christian* question: how do we who have been claimed by and who profess faith in Jesus Christ account for and understand the reality of religious diversity in the world? This chapter represents the first stage in answering this question, based on a survey of the Old Testament. In the next two chapters, we will consider this question in the gospels and Acts.

Four conclusions can be drawn from our review of the Old Testament narrative: (1) there is one family of humankind; (2) God is in covenant relationship with all humankind through Noah; (3) diversity of language and culture (and by extension, religion) is God's plan not God's punishment; and (4) God is present to and active in the lives of persons and nations outside of Israel.

1. The narrative of Genesis presents the view that all humanity shares a common ancestry. All creation has one source; everything that exists comes from God, who made it. All life and life of all kinds has its common origin in God alone. There is no second force at work. Creation is the result neither of the conflict nor of sexual activity between divine beings. At the beginning, there is only God.

The first account of creation (Gen. 1) is often called the Priestly version, divided as it is into six days and the Sabbath, and punctuated with various liturgical refrains ("and God said that it was good" and "there was evening and there was morning"). On the "sixth day," God created "everything that creeps upon the ground of every kind" (what we would call animals) and human beings. The creation of humanity is unique among all that God has done, for here God says, "Let us make humankind in our image, according to our likeness" (Gen. 1:26). Among all creation, it is the human creature that is designed to reflect the nature and being of God. Humanity is made with a correspondence to the God who made it. Theologians have reflected for millennia about what precisely this means. Since God is clearly understood to be a being not confined by the restrictions of a physical body, a literal, physical resemblance is ruled out: we don't *look* like God.

Many theories have been advanced about what being created in God's image means. Some have argued that we are like God in that we have a soul or spiritual essence. Others suggest that the resemblance is found in a particular human capacity or ability, such as the capacity for moral reasoning, ethical choice, and free will; the rational capacity or the ability to think, know, and understand; or the relational capacity, symbolized by being created male and female. The very simplicity of the text provides a number of ways in which to reflect on human nature as resemblance to the Creator. But a precise definition of this resemblance is less important than the implication of the larger context, namely, that all of humankind has one source, and all human beings share in being reflections of the divine origin.

What, then, of the diversity of human life (language, custom, culture, and religion)? The creation stories suggest that, whatever our differences, we share a common humanity because we share a common origin. Human difference can be understood only in the light of God's creative act that brought us all into existence in the first place. Everyone who ever has lived and everyone living today thus share a common origin and a common life. As creatures of one Creator, we are members of a single family and are expected to honor and respect all others who share as we do in the image and likeness of God. The Christian (and Jewish) understanding of creation and human origins thus leads us to conclude that all people (regardless of culture or ethnicity or religion) are members of our family, since we are all the offspring of the one God.

2. The covenant of God with humankind through Noah is the second critical text in any consideration of human and religious diversity. It is the first account of what the Bible understands to be God's distinctive way of relating to humanity. The stories of Jewish life and Christian faith are stories of covenant. Israel experienced God through a series of negotiated relationships, beginning with God's covenant with Abraham and culminating at Sinai. In each case, God reveals Godself as the one who makes and keeps promises, who claims people to be God's own, who expects loyalty and obedience from those people, and who promises loyalty to them forever. The relationship between God and humanity portrayed throughout the Bible is not a relationship of equality but one of reciprocity. God and humankind are not equal partners; but God does bind Godself and makes promises that cannot be broken.

The covenant with Noah is found in the "prehistory" of the Old Testament. Even though it includes genealogies and names some identifiable places, the story of Noah belongs to a mythic past. God has created the world and living creatures, but God is appalled by the evil and corruption that pervades God's human creation. Why did God not forsee this eventuality and take steps to prevent it? The Bible neither asks nor answers that question. The evil in the world is the backdrop for God's first venture in establishing covenant relations with humankind.

God's solution to the evil God sees is to wipe out all life except for a remnant of humans, animals, and birds that will be used to start all over again. God does this by singling out Noah and his family for a particular task and then for a special relationship. Noah, the text tells us, was a righteous and blameless man who "walked with God." To him is given the task of building the ark of refuge and selecting the various creatures to be saved. After the flood that destroys everything and everyone except those whom Noah has gathered, God reinstitutes the command made to the first humans: be fruitful and multiply and fill the earth. To this, God adds a command that forms the basis for ethical behavior: human beings may eat anything that moves (except the flesh or meat is not to be eaten with the "life" or blood in it). But if any animal or human takes the life of another human being, the life of that animal or human will be required in return. Sensing that violence and murder are the root of the human evil that occasioned the destruction, God now commands that human life be honored and preserved. The reason goes directly to creation itself: all are created in the image and likeness of God.

Then God does something quite surprising: God makes a promise to Noah and to all of Noah's descendants never again to destroy life by the waters of the flood. God is now obligated, and the object of God's obligation is the entire human family. Noah and his sons are the new beginning of the human race; thus God's covenant is with all people who will ever live.

This all-embracing covenant has several profound implications. First, it reinforces the belief in unity of all humanity as members of one family. Second, it is the story of a covenant of life that God makes, not with one "chosen people," but with humanity as a whole. Later, Israel will use the word *hesed* (steadfast love) to describe God's motivation for the subsequent covenants with Abraham and Moses, but it is not too much to say that the covenant with Noah represents God's steadfast love for the creation and in particular for God's human family. What follows in the story of Abraham echoes this theme. There God promises to bless all humankind through Abraham. But here the scope is intentionally wider. All persons and all living creatures exist under God's blessing and protection.

This ancient covenant with Noah is followed by others that are more specific in terms of the people chosen and in which the obligations they take on increase. How do we read these in relation to one another? It would be easy to think that the covenants that God makes are sequential, stepping stones that move from less to greater specificity, from less to greater fullness, from partial to more complete truth. Christians in particular have been tempted to read the covenants in this way, and specifically to say that the "new covenant" in Jesus Christ "supersedes" all that has gone before. This has led many Christians to think that Christianity now replaces all other religions in general and Judaism in particular. But the Bible does not make this claim. The Old Testament does not read the covenants with Noah, Abraham, and Moses in this way. Paul specifically takes up this question in Romans 9–11 with respect to the "new covenant": "I ask then, has God rejected his people? By no means!" (Rom. 11:1). In recent years, Christian theologians have come to argue that the notion of "supersessionism" (the idea that each "old" covenant is replaced by the next) is bad theology because it imagines that God could go back on God's promises.

The view that has replaced this, which directly applies Paul's argument, is that God's promises given in the past remain in force today. This has been especially important for Jewish-Christian relations, for it has allowed Christians to come to the view that all are saved through the promises of God, whether those made through the covenant at Sinai or the new covenant in Christ. Because God is one, God's promises must also be one. We will return to the particular issue of Christianity and Judaism in the next chapter when we consider the question of religious diversity and the person of Jesus Christ. For now, the important point is the unity and continuity of the divine covenants.

This view of the continuity of God's promise in fact leads to a reading quite the opposite of supersessionism. If the God who makes and keeps promises is the same God in all ages, then each successive covenant should be seen in light of the one or ones that have gone before. If the covenant with Noah, a covenant that promises (on God's part) and requires (on humanity's part) the protection of life, is made with all humanity, then the more specific covenants (especially Sinai and the "new covenant") can rightly be seen as specific elaborations or ways of living out the covenant God has made with the whole human race.

3. This brings us to the question of how to understand the diversity of human ethnicity, culture, and even religion. Where do the variety and continuing vitality of human culture fit into God's providence? As we saw in considering the story of the tower of Babel, one traditional interpretation is that the scattering of humanity and the differentiation of languages was punishment for human sin. According to early interpreters of this story, the crime that could justify God's intervention was the building of the tower, which was seen as an "assault" on heaven, an invasion of God's territory.[5]

There are at least two problems with this reading. First, this interpretation sees the "scattering" as punishment rather than as the original plan. If in fact God's original intention was that humans should multiply and fill the earth, then spreading out is the logical and obvious way that this would take place. The key to this interpretation is to read the tower of Babel in light of the creation command (Gen. 1:28) and the reiteration of that command to Noah's family after the flood (Gen. 9:1). As Hiebert suggests, the sin of humanity is the instinct to stay together, to find unity in uniformity rather than in God's intended diversity.

The second problem that the traditional interpretation presents is its view of the divine motivation. What does it suggest about the nature of God if what God is doing is thwarting an "invasion" of God's territory? We no longer think about God as having a "territory" that is God's refuge apart from the creation, for indeed the whole universe belongs to God and is God's good creation. Further, the God who is the creator of all is unlikely to be capable of being "threatened" by the creature. The traditional interpretation turns the tower building into a moral problem: humans have overstepped the boundary between Creator and creature. But, as Hiebert has shown, one has to import that theological idea into the text itself. The more straightforward reading is preferable because it is actually more consistent with the view of a God who out of God's own being brought all things into being, called everything good and made human beings to share in the divine vocation of tending or caring for creation.

To be sure, the diversity of languages and cultures has led to great misunderstandings and to competition for scarce resources such as land, water, and oil. But it can be argued that the problem is not the diversity itself, but rather the human unwillingness to reach across the barriers difference sometimes creates and to embrace the other as members of one family. To take an analogy from the rest of creation, one of the miracles of life is the enormous variety and adaptation of plant and animal life to the many different habitats on earth. Far from being a drawback, this variety is what makes life possible.

4. This takes us to the theological question: is it possible that the different human cultures and their religions are something like human adaptations to differing environments? Just as the diversity of plant life and animal species is part of God's plan for thriving creation, perhaps the diversity of religious life is part of how God has been present to all of God's human creation for millennia. At least this view is more consistent with our conviction that God loves all beings than the idea that God has been (and/or is) present only to one part of the human family.

The possibility that the diversity of humankind is part of God's providential plan finds support in various Old Testament writings. It is clear that God has plans for other nations or peoples besides Israel. In the story of Abraham, God promises to bless the descendants of Ishmael as well as Isaac (Gen. 17:20 and 21:18). Two nations and two religious traditions come from God's gift of life through Abraham. In the writings of the prophets, we find evidence that God uses the actions of other nations for God's purposes in relation to Israel (e.g., "Thus says the LORD to his anointed, to Cyrus, whose right hand I have grasped" Isa. 45:1). The prophet even has a vision of Egypt and Assyria (Israel's enemies and oppressors) as inheritors with Israel of God's blessing: "Blessed be Egypt my people, and Assyria the work of my hands, and Israel my heritage" (Isa. 19:25).

What can we conclude from this reflection on Old Testament sources? The main concept we have considered in this chapter is the larger plan or purposes of God. While in no way denying the specificity of God's covenant with Israel, a fuller reading suggests that this covenant of particularity exists within God's larger plan for the whole of creation, which includes the variety of human nations, cultures, and religions. How this diversity of humankind is understood in relationship to God's new covenant in Jesus Christ is the topic of the next chapter.

3

At the Name of Jesus

Without doubt the most challenging aspect for Christians living with religious diversity is the tension between the affirmation of God's love for all creation and all people and the confession that Jesus Christ is Savior and Lord. How do we make both of these claims at the same time? How do these two ideas hold together? We see the tension reflected in our hymns: "There's a wideness in God's mercy, like the wideness of the sea," but "at the name of Jesus every knee shall bow, every tongue confess him King of glory now."

I believe that these two ideas must always be affirmed together. The fullness of Christian faith requires affirming both the universal range of God's love and the particular confession that it is through Jesus Christ that this love is fully known and experienced. Failure to hold these two ideas together leads to serious theological problems. To hold only the first view is to lose the insight and experience of relationship to God through Christ that makes Christian faith distinctive. To hold the second view without the first forecloses God's sovereign freedom to love and save whomever God chooses. The first idea held alone ignores the claims of the New Testament about the nature and person of Jesus Christ. The second idea without the first is equally unfaithful to the sovereign freedom of God's grace and the indelibility of God's promises that we explored in the previous chapter. Only by holding the universality and particularity of Christian faith together can Christians approach an adequate understanding of how to relate to other faith traditions and those who follow them. How it is possible to do this will be the task of this chapter.

In the first chapter, I noted the significant role that context plays in shaping theological understandings and expression. That is, the situation in which the community of faith finds itself plays a major role in determining both what theological issues will be considered important or urgent and how those theological ideas will be expressed. Christian faith has always been aware of the issue of Christian confession in the context of other faith traditions. Indeed, Christianity began as a movement within Jewish faith and practice and only gradually became differentiated into a distinct religion. As Christians spread their faith in the Gentile world, they explained their faith in the context of the great religious diversity of the Roman Empire. Much of the earliest theological writing in the church attempted to explain Christian practices and defend them against criticism from those who followed other, at the time more dominant, religious traditions.

Early theologians were open to the possibility that those who lived before Christ and some who followed other paths could be saved. But the dominant theological view came to be what we have identified as Christian exclusivism. The view that eventually prevailed can be summed up in the famous phrase of Cyprian, bishop of Carthage (d. 258) in North Africa: *extra ecclesiam nulla salus* (outside the church there is no salvation). Cyprian stated this principle as a response to internal conflict in the church and delivered it as a warning to Christians who had left the main body of believers to follow a schismatic group. After Christianity became the official religion of the Roman Empire under Constantine, however, this view was applied to Jews and "pagans" (i.e., those who followed traditional Greco-Roman religions or quasi-religious philosophical schools).[1] Later, when the church had social approval with political power behind it, the exclusivist position became a way to enforce Christian orthodoxy on dissenters, those within the church, as well as those on the outside.

After Europe became an essentially Christian culture, those who followed other religious traditions either became an oppressed minority (for example, Jews) or were identified as foreign enemies (for example, Muslims). Only after the age of exploration began did European Christians encounter a wider diversity of religious traditions, and several eras of missionary activity followed, in which the foremost goal was conversion. In the modern period, three conditions have come together to make the fact of religious diversity a theological problem in a new way. First, established Christian churches now exist in nations where other religions are very strong or dominant traditions (e.g., in various parts of Africa and Indonesia where Islam is strong, in the Indian subcontinent, where Hinduism is dominant, and parts of Asia where Buddhist and Confucian traditions shape the culture). This experience of diversity has given rise to Christian theological reflection that is shaped by appreciation as well as critique of differing religious traditions.

Second, changes in immigration laws have led to the presence of large communities of non-Christians (notably Muslims, Hindus, and Buddhists) in both Europe and North America. This means that those who follow other religions are no longer only objects of mission far away but next door neighbors, coworkers, and friends. Third, the era of instant communication means greater awareness of people, their cultures and situations, and the role religion plays in conflicts in various regions (the Middle East, India, Northern Ireland, to name a few).

These various situations make us ask the question of Christian faith and religious diversity in new ways. Our new reality makes us wonder whether being Christian means claiming that we are right about God and everyone else is wrong. When diversity of religious life and practice is part of everyday life,

Christians are led to ask whether the traditional Christian claim that only we are saved and all others are condemned or damned is the only faithful alternative. At the heart of the matter is what we believe about the person and work of Jesus Christ and how we believe God is revealed through his life, death, and resurrection.

RETHINKING FAMILIAR TEXTS

The best place to begin this consideration is with those New Testament texts that seem most clearly to present the "exclusivist" view. The confession that Jesus is both Savior and Lord is at the heart of the New Testament; it is, in fact, the message. But two passages are lifted up most frequently when the topic of religious diversity is raised. We will look at them both and consider whether looking at them in their larger context helps broaden our understanding of their meanings.

The most frequently cited passage is John 14:6: "I am the way, and the truth, and the life. No one comes to the Father except through me." The passage seems very straightforward: Jesus is the only point of access to God the Father; Jesus is "the truth" about God; Jesus is the one through whom people will come to have eternal life.

The first thing to be said about this passage is that it is a statement about Jesus' identity, not a statement about other religions. Most often, however, the statement is read to support the claim that if Jesus (and by extension, Christianity) is "the way," then there are no other "ways." But that is an extension of the statement and goes beyond what is claimed in the words themselves. The text says what Jesus *is*; it does not say what anything else *is not*.

The most important issue, however, is to look at the context of this one verse. The setting is the meal Jesus has with his disciples shortly before his betrayal and arrest. Chapters 14–17 of John's Gospel are often called "the farewell discourse." Jesus is portrayed as speaking almost without interruption and, using a variety of images and metaphors, giving his final instructions and thoughts to the disciples. Chapter 14 begins with Jesus' statement that "in my Father's house there are many dwelling places" (14:2). He says that he is going there to prepare a place for the disciples who will join him there later. He concludes by saying, "And you know the way to the place were I am going" (14:4). The reader knows that Jesus is talking about his impending death and resurrection. The reader also knows that Jesus has come from God and is returning to God (John 13:3).

The disciples, however, (whose role is to misunderstand and thus to raise questions) say, "We do not know where you are going. How can we know the way?" (14:5). Jesus' response is a classic example of how John portrays Jesus speaking on one level of meaning (metaphorical) while his conversation partner is hearing on another (usually literal). If you think Jesus is talking about a path or some other literal form of journey, no wonder you are confused when he responds, "*I* am the way." What the larger context indicates is that Jesus, speaking of his coming death and resurrection, is announcing that he is returning to God, from whom he came, and that now he himself (on the other side of death and resurrection) will be the "way" that the disciples must follow (by faith, but also perhaps by imitation). In this sense, the passage is something like the familiar saying from the Synoptic Gospels, "If any want to become my followers, let them deny themselves and take up their cross and follow me" (Matt. 16:24).

Another meaning of this passage involves Jesus' naming of God as "my Father." This language is peculiar to John's Gospel. Here a new insight into the being of God is being formed as Jesus and God are called Son and Father. In fact, the father language for God here is not generic (suggesting that God is "like a father"); rather, this language is employed to frame a radically new insight into the being of God. Eventually, this insight will be developed into the doctrine of the Trinity, the view of God that makes Christianity unique. God is one and also at the same time three. In theologian Eberhard Jüngel's phrase, God is a being structured as a relationship. The one God is Father and Son and Spirit. In this sense, Jesus *is* the way in the specific sense of being the way into a unique understanding of God as the Father of the Son; he is the way into the triune nature of God. To shift the metaphor, Jesus is the window onto the Trinity, the one through whom we see into the mystery of God's triune life.

While this powerful statement in John's Gospel is about the "true" nature of Jesus and what his life, death, and resurrection reveal about God, it is not the answer to the specific question, "What is the status of other religions and those who follow them?" It is an affirmation of how Christians understand the person of Jesus Christ and the way in which that fundamentally changes our understanding of God. But that is not to answer the question of whether this is the *only* vision of God humanity can or will ever have.

Another text that receives a great deal of attention whenever the Christian understanding of religious diversity is raised is Acts 4:12: "There is salvation in no one else, for there is no other name under heaven given among mortals by which we must be saved." Once again the context is critical to an appropriate understanding and use of the text. In Acts 4 Peter and John have been arrested for continuing to preach about Jesus' resurrection and have now been brought before the high priest and other religious leaders. In giving account of their faith, they are specifically defending the healing of a man unable to walk (3:1–10). In Greek the same word can be translated both "made whole (or healed)" and "saved." The physical and "spiritual" are two aspects of one reality. And the "name" or authority by which this healing took place, Peter proclaims, is that of Jesus of Nazareth. Beverly Gaventa points out that the phrase "by which we must be saved" sounds a bit strange in English. It is an attempt to render the Greek *dei*, "it is necessary." Luke in particular uses this word for things that happen in accordance with God's will. The force of Peter's claim is that it is through God's will that the name of Jesus brings healing or salvation. Thus Gaventa concludes, "In context, the emphasis falls on God's gift of salvation rather than on a negation of other religious practices."[2] This text *does* make a powerful claim about the healing/saving power of the name of Jesus. It does not necessarily mean that God could not or would not work in the lives of human beings by other means.

This section has looked at two particularly important New Testament texts that are often cited in discussing the Christian approach to religious diversity. My goal has been to show something of what those verses mean in their contexts. I do not deny the validity of either text, but rather suggest that neither one was originally intended as an answer to the question of the relation of Christianity to other religions. There are other places in the New Testament where religious diversity appears, however, and they should be examined with care.

THE RELIGIOUS "OTHERS" IN THE GOSPELS

Much of the New Testament is colored by the polemical situation in which the early Christians found themselves. Jesus, all of his disciples, and almost all the earliest believers were Jews. Modern scholars (both Jewish and Christian) suggest that the best way to understand the early church is to see it as a reform movement within Judaism that within a couple of generations broke away to form its own distinctive religious community. Indeed, many scholars say that Christianity and modern Judaism are both religious responses to the destruction of the temple in Jerusalem in AD 70. Thus, in particular, passages in the Gospels that portray "the Jews" in very negative terms are best understood as the result of strained and angry relations internal to the Jewish community, not as blanket condemnations of either Jews in general or other religions as a whole.

Alongside the texts that present an "exclusive" stance towards others there are other places in the gospel story that present a different picture. When we ask where the religious "other" (that is, non-Jews or Gentiles) appears in the story of Jesus and how the religious "other" is portrayed, we find some perhaps surprising answers. These passages can also give guidance to us on how we might approach religious diversity and relate to those of other religious traditions today.

The Gospel of Luke is characterized by the significant number of passages in which the religious "others" are cast in a very positive light. Luke's overall point in the Gospel is to lay the groundwork for his history of the early Christian movement in the Acts of the Apostles and thus to provide an implicit defense of the "mission to the Gentiles." His theme in both the Gospel and Acts is that the good news of the reign of God is for Gentiles as well as Jews. But in addition to this "inclusive" theological message, the way Luke portrays Gentiles suggests something about how we might understand religious diversity in our own day.

The positive light in which Gentiles are seen is obvious from the beginning. Luke addresses his work to Theophilus (literally, God-lover). He could already be a believer, or perhaps he is a "God-fearer," a non-Jew who respected the religion of Israel. The theme of the Gospel with respect to the Gentiles is voiced early on in the song of Simeon, the old man who blesses the infant Jesus in the temple shortly after his birth. Simeon praises God for allowing him to see the fulfillment of God's promise, "a light for revelation to the Gentiles and for glory to your people Israel" (Luke 2:32).

Luke sets the stage in Jesus' ministry for outreach to the Gentiles during his first sermon in Nazareth (Luke 4:16–30). After announcing the theme of his ministry with words from Isaiah, Jesus makes the startling statement "no prophet is accepted in the prophet's hometown." He then cites two famous incidents from Israel's history when God, through the prophets Elijah and Elisha, reached out to persons beyond the covenant community. In the first case, Elijah was sent to a widow in Sidon (Canaanite territory) and helped her survive during the terrible drought brought on by Israel's disloyalty to God (1 Kgs. 17:8–16). In the second, Elisha was sent to cure Naaman, leading general of the Syrian army, of leprosy (2 Kgs. 5). Here Jesus is calling on precedents in Israel's own history that show God's care and compassion for those outside the covenant with Abraham and Sarah. Israel may indeed be God's chosen, but the lives of these "others" are precious to God as well. God's promise to be Israel's God does not mean that God ceases to be the God of all humanity. Luke tells us that the good people of Nazareth were furious when they heard this, because they recognized in Jesus' words their own desire to see themselves as privileged by being "related" to Jesus in a special way. As we will see, this theme, of supposedly knowing whom God favors and whom God does not, will occur again in this Gospel.

The most extended incident in Luke between Jesus and an "outsider" is found in chapter 7, the healing of the Roman centurion's servant. This soldier bears a great resemblance to Cornelius in Acts 10. Both are part of the Roman army of occupation. From the Jewish point of view, these Romans are religiously off-limits. They are representatives of the oppression and political subjugation of their nation. At the same time, however, they are portrayed as benefactors of the local communities: "It is he who built our synagogue for us," the elders say as they appeal to Jesus on the soldier's behalf (Luke 7:5).

When Jesus sets out to the soldier's home to heal the servant, he is met by a delegation bringing a message from the soldier: "Lord, do not trouble yourself, for I am not worthy to have you come under my roof; therefore I did not presume to come to you. But only speak the word, and let my servant be healed. For I am also a man set under authority, with solders under me; and I say to one, 'Go,' and he goes, and to another 'Come,' and he comes, and to my slave, 'Do this,' and the slave does it" (vv. 6–8). Jesus recognizes immediately that this Roman soldier understands Jesus' own relationship to the divine authority he represents. "Not even in Israel have I found such faith," Jesus says (v. 9). The clear implication is that the ability to recognize the presence and power and goodness of God is not limited to the chosen people. The religious "others" are not prevented from knowing God even if they do not know or practice the religion of Israel.

When Matthew recounts the same incident, Jesus adds this: "I tell you, many will come from east and west and will eat with Abraham and Isaac and Jacob in the kingdom of heaven, while the heirs of the kingdom will be thrown into the outer darkness, where there will be weeping and gnashing of teeth" (Matt. 8:11–12). On the one hand, this text presents the troubling theme of the "replacement" of Israel as God's chosen. On the other hand, it makes clear the theme that the reign of God extends beyond the covenant as Israel understood it at the time.

The question of how far the grace or mercy of God extends or to whom the message of the good news is open is a critical question as well for the Gospel of Matthew. One incident in particular illumines this tension, not only in the life and ministry of Jesus, but also in the community for whom Matthew was writing. The incident recounted in Matthew 15:21–28 has Jesus and the disciples journeying outside of Israel geographically as well as religiously. In the region of Tyre and Sidon, they are accosted by a Canaanite woman who begs Jesus to heal her daughter. Jesus replies with an "exclusive" interpretation of his mission: "I was sent only to the lost sheep of the house of Israel" (v. 24). Such a statement would have reflected the view that Jesus had come as a "reformer" of Jewish faith. But when the woman continues to plead with Jesus, he responds with one of the most chilling statements recorded in any Gospel: "It is not fair to take the children's food and throw it to the dogs." The woman is as undaunted as she is persistent and makes the sharp comeback, "Yes, Lord, yet even the dogs eat the crumbs that fall from their masters' table" (v. 27).

It is as though Jesus himself then sees not only this individual woman but the whole matter of his mission in a new light. This Gentile woman, this religious "outsider," has pressed Jesus to rethink how far the mercy of God extends. By turning an insult into a metaphor, she lays claim to the universal scope of God's grace and to God's freedom to heal whomever God chooses.

Another intriguing example of the role of the religious "other" in the Gospels is found in the various ways in which Samaritans are portrayed. Samaritans, who lived in the region between Judea and the Galilee, followed a form of Jewish life at odds with the dominant practice centered around the Jerusalem temple. Generally speaking, they were seen as enemies or outcasts by the dominant Judaism, and references to them in other writings of the time are very derogatory. Portraying them in a positive light was a bold move both for Jesus and the Gospel writers. First, one of the most famous of Jesus' parables concerns the "good Samaritan" (Luke 10:25–37). Our unfamiliarity with the tension between Jews and Samaritans blunts the point of the story. Jesus is not only making a point about what it means to be a neighbor to another (namely, to reach out to someone in need). The drama of the story lies in the irony that it is not the religious officials (the priest and the Levite) but rather the religious "other" who is hated by Jesus' audience who stops to render aid and fulfills the command to love one's neighbor as oneself.

The second incident comes from the Gospel of John, which records Jesus' extended conversation with the woman at the well (John 4). Jesus and the disciples are traveling through Samaria. The disciples leave Jesus at a village well while they go off to buy food for the midday meal. A woman comes to draw water, and Jesus engages her in conversation that ranges from spiritual nourishment to the religious differences between Jews and Samaritans to the woman's own life. At the end, she goes off to tell her neighbors what has happened to her, and they too come to welcome Jesus and to receive his teaching. Here Jesus has no hesitancy to engage someone from outside the religious boundaries of his faith community. Indeed, he reaches out to her with respect and compassion.

What can we say about the place of the religious "other" in the Gospels? What insights might we draw from these texts for our situation today? I believe there are three. First, these passages build on the theme we found in the Old Testament, namely, that God's mercy and grace, while promised to Israel, are not confined to the chosen people. By extrapolation, then, we may question whether it is right to say that Christians have exclusive claim to the goodness and love of God. The fact that God has chosen to reveal Godself to Christians in the person of Jesus Christ does not necessarily mean that God thereby closes off relationship with all others. While Jews and Christians are to be "exclusive" in their loyalty to God and forgo allegiance to other "gods" or ideologies, God is free to be "inclusive," because all people still belong to God and are equally creatures of the one Creator.

Second, knowledge of God seems not to be limited to Israel and to Christians. While it is clear that God speaks to Israel in clear and decisive ways, and while Christians claim that God is manifested uniquely and fully through Jesus Christ, nevertheless the Bible gives ample evidence that others can and do recognize the presence and power of God. Christian theology has traditionally talked about this by making a distinction between "special" versus "general" revelation. All persons can know God as Creator through "general revelation," as they observe the universe and as they exercise their individual conscience. What the church has received and believers follow is the "special revelation" or "saving knowledge" of God in Jesus Christ. Where this distinction is employed (as it is in Roman Catholic theology), it provides a way for Christians to find common ground with persons from differing religious traditions and practices. In fact, this distinction allows for one theological understanding of other religions, that is, as the product of the universal human attempt to respond to and understand the Creator.

Protestants, especially those who follow the theology of John Calvin, have generally dismissed this distinction and argued that the effects of sin are such that humans can never have true knowledge of God apart from God's revelation in Jesus Christ and Scripture. Karl Barth, noted twentieth-century theologian, argued that one must distinguish between religion (the human attempt to know God) and revelation (God's self-disclosure). On these terms, all religion (including the Christian) is fatally flawed and prone to idolatry. Only God's own Word (Jesus Christ) imparts true knowledge of God. On the one hand, this position draws attention to the limited character of all human knowledge and to the pervasive power of sin as self-deception (thinking we know what is true or good when in fact we do not). But at the same time, this emphasis on human limitation and sinfulness seems to exclude evidence within the

Bible itself of human awareness of God (especially in nature) and of those outside the covenant who are deemed to be "righteous" or "wise," and thus have come to know at least something of how to live so as to please God.

The third thing that can be said on the basis of this reading of the Gospels is that God's compassion for human suffering extends beyond the covenant relationship between God and Israel. This is precisely the point that Jesus made in his sermon at Nazareth in Luke's Gospel. Many widows in Israel were destitute and on the point of death during the drought; many lepers in Israel were in need of healing and restoration; but the prophets were sent, by the mercy of God, to the "others," to Gentile sufferers. In the healing of the centurion's slave, Jesus acts out this vision. The mercy and compassion of God extend beyond the "primary relationship" between God and God's chosen people.

Even though the precedent for this view was already present in Jewish tradition, the difficulty for the early church (and perhaps even for Jesus) of accepting its implications is evident in the story of the Canaanite woman who begs for her daughter's healing. This powerful story on one level suggests a broadening of Jesus' own understanding of his mission and thus of God's plan. On another level, it surely represents the conflict in the early church about the appropriateness of the mission to the Gentiles.

It would be a mistake to think that we have moved beyond this problem of how broadly to understand the extent of God's love. Some years ago, a leading evangelical Protestant leader preached a sermon declaring that God does not hear the prayers of Jews because they do not pray in the name of Jesus. One of the implications of such a statement is that God does not care about the concerns, needs, and cares of Jews (or others) in the same way God cares about those of Christians. The preacher doubtless intended to make a statement about "false" versus "true" religion, but by phrasing it the way he did, he made a claim about the limits of God's compassion. I hope this review of the biblical witness makes such a view untenable. For human beings to pretend to know the limits of God's love is the height of human arrogance. To attempt to confine the grace and mercy of God to one's own religious community is not only selfish; it is to claim to know what simply cannot be known.

WHO CAN BE SAVED?

Having examined the role of the religious "other" in the Gospels, we have found substantial support for the theological affirmation of the universal scope of God's love. Now we must return to the other theological affirmation that must be held in tension with it if one is to be consistent with Christian tradition. We confess that Jesus Christ is both Savior and Lord and that God wills to save humankind through him. This is the core of the Christian confession. But now we ask: What does this have to do with how we think about those who follow other religious traditions? How is our understanding and articulation of this confession to be shaped by our experience of living in a religiously plural world?

The traditional way of asking this question is: Can non-Christians be saved? And if so, how is that possible? Does God save only those who profess explicit faith in Christ as Savior and Lord? These questions lead to others: What about all the people who lived and died before the time of Jesus? What about those who have lived since but have never come in contact with the gospel? What about children who die before they are baptized or make a profession of faith? While none of these is a completely new question, the contemporary situation has pressed them upon Christian communities with new urgency.

A number of approaches have been explored by different branches of the church. In *Nostra Aetate* ("Declaration on the Relation of the Church to Non-Christian Religions"), Vatican II urges that Christians approach all persons as members of the one family of God and be ready to recognize and welcome the truth that is found in other religions, while nevertheless proclaiming "the cross of Christ as the sign of God's universal love and the source of all grace."[3] In its document on the church (*Lumen Gentium*), the council affirms that those who "through no fault of their own" seek to know God and to live according to God's will as they understand it "may attain eternal salvation."[4] As noted above, these positions build on and are fully in accord with the way Roman Catholic theology has understood general revelation.

Salvation has recently gained new attention in Protestant evangelical circles. In chapter 1, I referred to Clark Pinnock who has put forward a case for being "optimistic" rather than "pessimistic" about the extent of God's salvation. More recently, Terrance Tiessen has put forward a long and careful argument that shifts the emphasis in the discussion of salvation from the individual who makes the confession to God who desires that all should be saved (1 Tim. 2:4).[5] Each of these approaches has light to shed on this critically important topic.

In order to talk about the status of non-Christians, however, we need to discuss the meaning of salvation. Christians have understood this concept in many different ways. In fact, the idea and the experience are so rich that no one formulation or metaphor is truly sufficient. A good place to begin is with Paul's use of the term "reconciliation": "in Christ, God was reconciling the world to himself" (2 Cor. 5:19). Embedded in this concept is the claim that humanity is separated from God, that our relationship with God has been broken as a consequence of our sin, and that God provides the means (in Christ) for the restoration of that relationship. This suggests that salvation is not escape from punishment but rather restoration to the relationship of unity or communion that God desired for humanity from the beginning. In this sense atonement is "at-one-ment," bringing us and God back together. Salvation is thus both individual and communal, as expressed in Jesus' prayer for his disciples, "that they may be one, as we are one, I in them and you in me, that they may become completely one" (John 17:22–23). The object of salvation (in both John's Gospel and Paul's letters) is the whole world, indeed all of creation. It is not simply a question of whether or not you or I are saved, but God's intention for the whole world.

The role of Jesus in God's work of reconciliation or salvation is expressed in many different ways. One way to say it is this: Jesus shows us that God's name is Love. The life, teaching, ministry, death, and resurrection of Jesus show the world God's self-giving love, the love that empties itself for the healing of creation, that is poured out for the sins of the world (see Phil. 2). When humanity acknowledges God as Creator, we confess that everything belongs to God, that all that is comes from and returns to the one source of life. In Jesus Christ, Christians believe that the Creator is also the Redeemer, the one who comes to transform us and call us home. The God whose work is reconciliation is dramatically on display in the hospitality of Jesus, in eating with outcasts and sinners, in healing and restoring those outside the boundaries of society, and in welcoming his friends into a community of love. Salvation then is receiving the grace of God to be able to follow the way of Jesus, to live as he lived, full of love for God and neighbor.

So, will only those who "believe in Jesus" be saved? What about the others? Once again, the Christian tradition has offered various answers. These views of salvation can be characterized, most simply, in three ways: as "subjectivist," "participationist," and "objectivist." Obviously this is an oversimplification, but the categories are useful in looking at the range of responses based on different readings of Scripture.

1. The "subjectivist" view places the emphasis on the faith or personal commitment of the individual. The question, "when did you receive Jesus Christ as your personal Lord and Savior?" comes from this view of salvation. The effects of God's saving work in Jesus Christ are valid only for those who accept it. In the same way, those who reject God's message through Christ will be condemned. According to this view, salvation depends on the act of faith of the believer, and it is possible to reject or refuse God. Support for this position can be found in passages such as John 3:18: "Those who believe in him are not condemned; but those who do not believe are condemned

already, because they have not believed in the name of the only Son of God."

The effect of this view in relation to the question of religious diversity is rather straightforward. If salvation depends on the response of the individual believer, then all those who lived before Christ, all those who have never heard the gospel, and all those who (even having heard) have chosen to follow other religious practices are condemned and will not inherit eternal life. The zeal that many Christians have to share the gospel and convert others grows out of their sincere compassion for others and desire that they should be spared certain eternal death, which according to this view will be their ultimate fate.

There are two problems with this view. First, it is difficult to understand why God would have created humanity in God's own image and then condemned so much of humankind to eternal damnation. Presuming that God created out of love and continues to love all whom God made, it is hard to explain why God would leave so many of God's beloved without even the possibility of salvation. Second, this view suggests that human beings are able to resist God's will or intention, which puts the individual at the center of the equation: it is up to *me* to decide, rather than God.

2. The "participationist" view attempts to bring God's role in salvation and that of humanity into a kind of balance. On this view, human beings are "justified by faith," but faith means trusting in the promise of God and accepting what God has already done for humankind through the death and resurrection of Christ. Salvation is what God has already accomplished through Christ, and this salvation becomes effective in our lives when we accept it through faith and trust. This is made real to believers through baptism, in which we share (or participate in) the death of Christ, so that we may share in the new life with Christ. Some who articulate this view say that even saving faith is the work of God in the life of the believer.

The impact of this view on our understanding of those who follow other traditions is more difficult to judge. On the one hand, to the extent that this view emphasizes personal faith, we encounter the same problems described above. On the other hand, to the extent that it emphasizes salvation as the work God does through Christ, the question is rather more open as to who then receives the effects of that work. In fact, Paul argues that the model for "justification by faith" is Abraham, who trusted in God's promise. Obviously Abraham's faith was not in Jesus Christ but in the God who spoke directly to him. This view would seem to leave open the question of whether God might be at work in the lives of others who similarly "have faith" in the sense of trusting in God's promises as they understand them.

3. According to the "objectivist" understanding of salvation, salvation is entirely the work of God. It is the work God has been engaged in since the foundation of the world. Redemption or salvation through Christ is not God's Plan B, implemented when the original plan failed due to human sin. Rather, redemption and creation are two manifestations of the same love, two sides of one coin, two verses of the same song. The scope of redemption or salvation is precisely the same as creation itself; indeed the goal of salvation in Christ is the renewal and transformation of the universe. The plan is to "gather up all things in [Christ], things in heaven and things on earth" (Eph. 1:10). The whole creation is subject to "futility" (that is, to the effects of human sin), but "the creation itself will be set free from its bondage to decay and will obtain the freedom of the glory of the children of God" (Rom. 8:21).

Salvation is what God alone does, and whoever is saved, it is entirely of God's doing. Those of us who come to understand that this is what God is about in the world and trust in it by the power of the Spirit at work within us, are then enabled to live in accordance with God's purposes and experience the gifts of the Spirit in our lives. As Paul concludes, "By grace you have been saved through faith, and this is not your own doing; it is the gift of God—not the result of works, so that no one may boast" (Eph. 2:8–9).

What does this view of salvation mean for those who follow other religious traditions? Because this approach argues that the question of who is saved belongs finally and only to God, the question of who ultimately will be saved remains open. Because creation and redemption are seen as two aspects of the one plan or purpose of God, it is completely inappropriate for human beings to pretend to know how God will accomplish this work. We cannot and should not attempt to say whom God will save or how. What Christians can and should do is bear witness to God's love and live so as to give evidence of God's work in us.

Who then will be saved? The "objectivist" view says that this is finally up to God. This perspective is articulated succinctly in a catechism approved for study and use in the Presbyterian Church, "No one will be lost who can be saved. The limits of salvation, whatever they may be, are known to God. Three truths above all are certain. God is a holy God who is not to be trifled with. No one will be saved except by grace alone. And no judge could possibly be more gracious than our Lord and Savior, Jesus Christ."[6]

Each of these three ways of understanding the nature of salvation—the subjectivist, participationist, and objectivist—has different implications for the way we understand religious diversity. Each of them finds support in the Bible. Each of them makes one set of biblical passages the interpreter of the others. The advantage of the "objectivist" view is twofold. First, it provides a Christian theological basis for seeing God's work of salvation as inclusive of those who have followed and follow other religious traditions. Second, it keeps the emphasis in salvation exactly where it is with respect to creation. Both are the work of God. God is at the center of this picture, not humanity. And all human beings, Christian and non-Christian, are on the same footing as creatures of one Creator, whose plan is for the ultimate healing or renewal of creation.

CONCLUSION

This chapter began with a challenge: how can Christians confess Jesus Christ as Savior and Lord and at the same time affirm the universal love of God for all people, for all that God has made? I have argued here that these two are not ideas in tension but rather two sides of the same coin. Only in the context of God's universal love for all can the message of salvation in Christ be rightly understood; and it is precisely God's work in Christ that makes God's universal love visible and known. For Christians, these ideas belong together; this can never be either/or; it must always be both/and.

In this chapter, we began to explore the mystery of the Trinity as it is introduced by the unique relationship between the Father and the Son. In the next chapter, we turn to the work of the Holy Spirit and explore ways in which the triune being of God can be a model for understanding how God can be in relationship to all people.

4

Everywhere That We Can Be:
The Holy Spirit
and Religious Diversity

"Who has seen the wind?" asks poet Christina Rossetti. The poet concludes, as does Jesus (John 3:8), that we hear the sound of the wind and we see its effects, but we never see the wind itself. No wonder, then, that God is often understood through the metaphor of wind or breath. This is experience of God that is reflected when we speak of the Spirit of God or God the Holy Spirit. In this chapter I explore what Christian tradition has understood by God the Holy Spirit and how this understanding relates to our question of how Christians account for the religious diversity of humankind.

In the process, we will discover two side benefits of such a study. First of all, Western Christianity (in both mainline Protestant and Roman Catholic forms) has often been criticized for having a less-than-adequate understanding of the person and work of the Holy Spirit. This claim has long been made by theologians from the Eastern Orthodox traditions. In recent years, this sentiment has been voiced by the leaders of the now world-wide Pentecostal movement for whom the experience of the Spirit is at the heart of Christian faith and practice. Second, a discussion of the Holy Spirit will lead us into an explicit consideration of the Christian doctrine of the Trinity. As we will see, a number of theologians are now arguing that this distinctively Christian way of understanding God provides unanticipated avenues for an approach to understanding religious diversity.

THE SPIRIT AT WORK

In the languages of the Bible, both Hebrew and Greek, there is no distinctive word for "spirit" that is used to refer to God or a manifestation of God. Rather, what we translate as "Spirit" are two words, *ruach* (Hebrew) and *pneuma* (Greek), that are the ordinary words that mean either "wind" or "breath." This way of speaking about God and God's presence is rooted, on the one hand, in the equation of breath with life and, on the other hand, in the experience of wind as a powerful force of nature that provides the air that humans and animals breathe.

In the Old Testament, the Spirit of God is one of several manifestations of God or ways that God is God to Israel. Other examples include "the Word of the Lord," which provides the message to various prophets; "Wisdom" (in Greek, *Sophia*), who is portrayed as a force in creation and as one who guides human life; and the "glory of the Lord," which describes the outward or visible manifestation of the invisible God. Each of these at various times takes on an almost personal manifestation or is spoken of as a character alongside God.

It is sometimes difficult to distinguish between the literal and metaphorical use of *pneuma* or *ruach* in Scripture. For example, should the English translation of Genesis 1:2 speak of "a wind from God" or "the spirit of God" that sweeps over the face of the deep? Older translations chose "spirit" and by doing so reinforced the creedal notion of the role of the Holy Spirit in creation. The New Revised Standard Version and the standard Jewish English translation opt for "breath." This translation more accurately represents the literal meaning of the word and emphasizes that creation is God's own doing; God is not here working through a "manifestation."

Another reason for choosing "breath" in 1:2 is that it sets up the creation of human beings in Genesis 2:7, where the choice of "breath" is quite obvious: "Then the LORD God formed man from the dust of the ground, and *breathed* into his nostrils the *breath* of life" (emphasis added). Whichever English word is selected, however, the interplay between literal and metaphorical makes the point that God is the source of life itself and that all life comes from the creative force of God. Precisely the same "double meaning" comes into play in Psalm 104. The psalmist is praising God's work of creation and describes how all living creatures depend on God: "When you open your hand, they are filled with good things. When you hide your face, they are dismayed; when you take away their *breath* they die and return to their dust. When you send forth your *spirit*, they are created; and you renew the face of the ground" (Ps. 104:28b–30, emphasis added). These two different renderings of the same word reinforce the idea that all creatures that breathe depend on God's breath-spirit in order to live. (This kind of double meaning is also found in John 3, where Jesus employs the metaphor of wind [*pneuma*] to speak about being born "by water and the spirit" [*pneuma*].)

The personification of God's breath-spirit as the Spirit of God begins to be found in the later prophets, notably in Isaiah and Ezekiel. In Ezekiel's vision of the dry bones (representing the defeated and exhausted nation of Israel), God commands the prophet to "prophesy" and invoke the "breath" or Spirit to come upon the bones and give them life. Isaiah uses the metaphor of the spirit as the source of Israel's renewal (Isa. 32:15). It is the "spirit of the Lord" that commissions the messianic servant in Isaiah 61 to bring the good news of healing and release. Finally, the ultimate redemption of Israel is portrayed by Joel as the day when God says that "my spirit" will be poured out on all, young and old, women and men alike, and all will prophesy and have visions.

What ties these various uses of the "spirit" together is the idea that God is the one source of all life and the power upon which all life depends for its continued existence. Further, the Spirit of God is seen as the source of Israel's renewal or regeneration following the devastations of the exile. Through the Spirit, God is "giver of life" to all creation and "renewer of life" for God's people Israel.

When we turn to the New Testament, we notice that the Spirit has a much more prominent role, so much so that all the English translations capitalize the noun. While Paul prefers to speak simply of "the Spirit," the term "Holy Spirit" is found in the Gospels, especially in Luke. As we think about the chronology of these writings (Paul writing some thirty years prior to Luke), we can see a kind of theological evolution that sets the stage for the development of the doctrine of the Trinity, one God in three persons, Father, Son, and Holy Spirit. Among the Gospels themselves there is an intriguing variety of views regarding the Spirit. In the Gospel of John, Jesus makes reference to the Spirit during his ministry (especially in John 3 and 4), but he states clearly that the Spirit will come into the lives of the disciples only after Jesus himself has left them (see John 15 and 16). In Luke, by contrast, the Holy Spirit is an active character in the narrative from the very beginning. The Spirit is the power by which Mary conceives the child Jesus; the Spirit descends on Jesus at his baptism and then leads him into the wilderness to confront temptation; and Jesus claims the anointing of the Spirit at the beginning of his ministry. This role of the Holy Spirit is so prominent in Acts that it might even be called the "Acts of the Holy Spirit."

A full survey of the way the New Testament or even the book of Acts understands the person and work of the Holy Spirit is beyond the scope of this book. We will consider here the way Acts portrays the work of the Spirit in relation to the religious "others," to those understood to be outside God's covenant people, Israel. A careful examination of these texts leads to the conclusion that Luke understands God to be at work in the lives of all people, not just those whom God has chosen as God's own. I will look at three examples that present people who are "seekers," who have religious practices of their own, and who are introduced to the gospel by building on what they already know. While the point of each of these encounters is a story of conversion, there is a tacit assumption in each case that God is already involved in the lives of these characters.

The first story is of the African court official, often called the Ethiopian eunuch (Acts 8:26–40). The text presents an intriguing picture of this man: he is a black African and a prominent man, serving as the secretary of the treasury for the queen of Ethiopia. He is himself wealthy or at least travels with the benefits of wealth (as evidenced by the chariot in which he rides). As one might expect of someone holding his office, he is literate. He is described as a eunuch. While castrated males often held significant official positions in the ancient world, castration would presumably have prevented his full inclusion in the people of Israel, had he sought to become a proselyte (see Deut. 23:1).

His religious interest is especially intriguing. According to the text, he has come to Jerusalem to worship. Some commentators argue that this indicates that he was in fact a proselyte, but since Gentiles were permitted in the outer court of the temple, his presence there does not necessarily lead to that conclusion.[1] What is clear, however, is that he had enough interest and sufficient means to acquire a scroll of the prophet Isaiah. This is what Philip hears him reading when he enters the scene.

As New Testament scholar Beverly Gaventa points out, the Ethiopian is clearly a religious *seeker*, but he is not seeking out the Christian faith. Nor is Philip seeking him. Philip is brought on the scene by the Holy Spirit, who instructs Philip to intercept the official in his chariot. Philip (led by the Spirit) uses the text from Isaiah to tell him the story of Jesus, after which the Ethiopian asks to be baptized. While the point of this story is the conversion and baptism of the official, the text makes it abundantly clear that this man was already a religious seeker in whom God was already at work, making him ready to hear the good news. The text also goes out of its way to emphasize what

an "unlikely suspect" this man was. He is an "other" to the faith
of Israel in so many ways: as an African, as a man of another
religious background, as a man of wealth and power, and as
what we might call a "sexual minority," one who was legally
excluded from full participation in the religious life of Israel.
But it is precisely this "other" to whom the Holy Spirit has
directed the messenger and for whom the Spirit has prepared
the way.

The second important story is that of Peter and Cornelius in
Acts 10. This extended incident sets the scene for a meeting of
the church in Jerusalem, at which Peter reports Cornelius's
conversion, and the door is opened to the expansion of Christian mission from the Jewish community to the Gentile world
(Acts 11:1–18). Once again, the point of the story is the conversion of a Gentile; but for our purposes here what is important to notice is the implicit understanding both of God's
intention to include the Gentile and of God's role in the lives
of these religious others before the time of their conversion.

We are introduced to Cornelius in the opening verses: "In
Caesarea there was a man named Cornelius, a centurion of the
Italian Cohort, as it was called. He was a devout man who
feared God with all his household; he gave alms generously to
the people and prayed constantly to God" (Acts 10:1–2). The
picture is quite detailed: a soldier of the Roman army of occupation, stationed at the large port city of Caesarea, Cornelius is
a "God-fearer," a term usually employed to describe Gentiles
who studied and to some extent followed the religion of Israel
without becoming proselytes. He is "observant" according the
Jewish piety in two important ways: he gives alms and he prays
regularly. Already this man has responded to the presence of
God in his life.

One day Cornelius has a vision of an angel who informs
him that his prayers and alms "have ascended as a memorial
before God" (v. 4). He is then instructed to send to Joppa for
Peter. Meanwhile Peter has a dream in which God shows him
animals, birds, and reptiles and commands the hungry Peter to
kill and eat. Peter protests that he has never eaten prohibited

(or unclean) food, to which the voice of God says, "What God has made clean, you must not call profane" (v. 15).

Peter is still puzzling over this vision when messengers from Cornelius arrive imploring him to come to Caesarea. When Peter arrives at Cornelius's home, he sees the point of his dream: those whom he previously considered outside the bounds of proper association are the very ones whom God has selected to receive his teaching. Cornelius then shares his vision and Peter responds: "I truly understand that God shows no partiality, but in every nation anyone who fears him and does what is right is acceptable to him" (vv. 34–35). After Peter has shared the story of Jesus, the Holy Spirit is poured out on all those listening. Convinced by the manifestation of the Spirit, Peter proceeds to baptize Cornelius and all of his household. Once again, the boundaries of God's promise as previously understood have been broken open. More are included than Peter had previously imagined.

Peter's statement in verses 34 and 35 is quite astonishing from at least one version of the religious perspective in which Peter was raised. Many Jews today would concur completely with this view and would affirm that others besides Jews are capable of knowing how God wants human beings to live and of following God's path. But the context of the story presents a more "exclusive" version of the faith of Israel, and Peter's declaration is seen as a turning point in understanding the purposes and mission of God. As in the story of the Ethiopian, the initiator of this encounter is God, not Peter or Cornelius. It is clearly God's purpose to expand the other characters' understanding of the extent of God's inclusive promise. Peter's statement goes further, to claim that while God's covenant relationship with Israel might be thought of as showing "partiality" to one particular group within the human family, in fact God is not "partial," based on race or culture or even religion; rather, God welcomes all who seek to know and to do "what is right."

In the final incident, we find Paul, already known as the apostle to the Gentiles, in Athens. He has been debating not only in the synagogues with Jewish leaders but also in the public arena with Epicurean and Stoic philosophers. His speech at the Areopagus has become almost a classic example of what is known as "apologetic theology." In this approach, the believer uses terms known to or used by another tradition to explain or defend Christian faith. Paul begins by recognizing the important place of religious observance in Athenian life and points to one altar in particular dedicated "to an unknown god." Paul says: "What therefore you worship as unknown, this I proclaim to you. The God who made the world and everything in it, he who is Lord of heaven and earth, does not live in shrines made by human hands" (Acts 17:23–24). Paul recognizes the instinct to reach out beyond the human sphere in search of the divine. Rather than condemn this practice as idolatry (although Romans 1 shows clearly that this is what Paul thinks it is), here he reaches out and uses what he sees in the Greek religious practice as a stepping stone to his proclamation of the gospel.

Paul goes on to use what are presented as quotations from Greek "poets" or philosophers that suit the way he wishes to talk about the creative power of God and how God has made all humanity "from one ancestor" (v. 26). From Paul's perspective, the stories of Genesis (both creation and the flood) stand behind this understanding of God and God's relationship to all humanity. But his rhetorical move is to draw on the religious views of his audience as a way to lay the foundation for the message of his preaching.

What are we to conclude from these stories from Acts? In each of these incidents we find evidence for a more expansive way to understand both God's intentions for all humanity and the variety of human religious experience. Even though the primary point of these passages has to do with conversion, they all contain certain assumptions about the human religious situation. First, all of these Gentile characters are already in some sort of relationship with God prior to hearing the Christian message: they are seekers, "God-fearers" in relation to the faith of Israel, or simply followers of other traditions. This implies that human beings are made to seek relationship to God and have the capacity for responding to the presence of the divine in their lives. Second, these "others" have not only the capacity to seek but also the ability to discover something of God's purposes. The Ethiopian and Cornelius are described as devout; Cornelius has been led to practices that mark him as a righteous man; the Greek poet-philosophers have taught things about God and creation that Paul affirms are true. Third, and perhaps most important, these texts imply that God has already been at work in the lives of these people in ways that are surprising to the apostles. In the story of Cornelius, it is Peter who most needs to be persuaded of the extent of God's involvement in the lives of the "others." Indeed, Peter's "conversion" on this matter becomes a turning point for the Christian mission.

These texts have become newly important for the Christian enterprise of missiology, or thinking about Christian mission and evangelization. In past eras Christians often talked about "taking Christ" to the nations and operated on the assumption that non-Christians were idol worshipers at best or totally bereft of God at worst. Careful examination of these passages from Acts, coupled with several generations of Christian encounters with people of other religious traditions and cultures, has led to a rather different view, one more in accord with these texts. Now missiologists talk about identifying those places in other cultures or another person's experience where one can see evidences of God's presence, and building a presentation of the gospel from that point. They attempt to identify values, ethical norms, and behaviors from the religious or cultural traditions of others that are in accord with the biblical ethic. They speak about the human longings for God and the ways in which the Christian gospel satisfies them. To be sure, these are apologetic "techniques." But they also represent a theological shift that affirms the presence of God to all people and recognizes signs of God's activity in religious traditions outside the Christian fold. One of the bases for this revision of thinking is a deeper understanding of the Holy Spirit, affirmed in the creed as "the Lord, the giver of life." If that is the role of the Spirit, it follows that this "work" continues after the initiation of creation, that God as Spirit is present to all, and that God indeed is the one in whom "we live and move and have our being" (Acts 17:28).

Evidence for this subtle but important shift in thinking can be seen by comparing the text of the Nicene Creed with a contemporary confession of the Presbyterian Church. The ecumenical translation of the Nicene Creed reads: "We believe in the Holy Spirit, the Lord, the giver of life. . . ." These words not only refer to the opening words of Genesis, but also confirm that creation is the "work" not only of God the Father but also of God the Holy Spirit. In writing a contemporary statement of the Reformed faith, the Presbyterian Church uses these words: "We trust in God the Holy Spirit, everywhere the giver and renewer of life."[2] The introduction of the word "everywhere" serves to underscore the continuing presence and activity of God wherever there is life. Wherever we see new life and life renewed, we are seeing the work of God the Holy Spirit. The implications of this for the question of religious diversity are significant. If the Holy Spirit can be found everywhere, in human culture and society as well as in the natural world, it is not too much to conclude that the Holy Spirit may be found at work in the religious life of people of other faiths. To say that the Spirit is everywhere, however, is not to say that every aspect of human life is a manifestation of the Spirit. For the Christian, there are clear criteria for identifying—or as Paul puts it, discerning—the Spirit. Because the Holy Spirit is the Spirit of the God revealed in Jesus Christ, the presence of the Spirit will be recognized in values, beliefs, and actions that are in accord with the love and justice of Jesus Christ. The biblical record we have reviewed here suggests strongly that we should expect to see such signs of God's activity in every culture and religious tradition, through the power of the Holy Spirit.

THE TRIUNE GOD AND RELIGIOUS DIVERSITY

Thus far we have identified various ways in which the question of religious diversity and the status of those who follow other religious traditions might be understood in light of how God and God's actions are described in Scripture. Having examined various aspects of the story of God from the Old Testament, the ministry of Jesus, and the testimony to the work of the Spirit in the New Testament, we are ready to consider the question in the light of the doctrine of the Trinity. At first glance, it would seem that the Christian confession of the triune nature of God would be the last place where one would find assistance in approaching the question of religious diversity.

Many, in fact, would see this part of Christian doctrine as an obstacle to be avoided or issue to be set aside. What could be more problematic for Christian dialogue with Jews and Muslims, for example, who hold firmly that there is only one God and that God is *one*? To be sure, the Trinity, the belief that God is one God in three persons, has often been seen as a dogmatic puzzle rather than as a lived reality of faith. In some branches of Protestant Christianity, the doctrine is downplayed; in many, it is simply overlooked. Often in both public worship and personal devotion, believers focus on one person (for example, on Jesus) to the virtual exclusion of the other two. But orthodox Christian faith is grounded in the incarnation, the belief that God became human in Jesus Christ, and in the conviction that this leads to an understanding of God's self-disclosure as one God in the intimate relationship of Son, Father, and Spirit. Rather than set this rich and powerful idea aside for the sake of interreligious dialogue, I suggest that we look again at the doctrine of the Trinity, to discover whether it suggests a potential for the positive assessment of religious diversity.

The doctrine of the Trinity is not explicitly stated or "taught" in Scripture. Rather, this way of speaking to and about God grew up in the church based on the experience of believers. To put it simply, all the first Christians were Jews. They believed sincerely that there is only one God and that God is one. But as they encountered Jesus—and especially as they experienced the risen Christ—they came to understand him as God's Son and to use for him words previously reserved for God, namely, Savior and Lord. Then believers experienced the outpouring of the Holy Spirit in their life as a community. The earliest witness to the Trinity comes from Paul's benedictions in his letters, notably 2 Corinthians 13:13: "The grace of the Lord Jesus Christ, the love of God, and the communion of the Holy Spirit be with all of you." The emerging practice of baptism in the name "of the Father and of the Son and of the Holy Spirit" (Matt. 28:19) is other evidence of the development of this triune vision of God.

As the centuries passed, the Christian community became more explicit about what it meant by this formulation. Through the doctrine of the Trinity, Christians confess that God is one and three at the same time: one God and three ways of being God simultaneously. God is Father *and* Son *and* Spirit at the same time. Spirit, Son, and Father are each distinct from the others, and yet each is fully God. Theologians have explored numerous analogies in an attempt to make this concept more understandable. Augustine (who wrote a treatise on the Trinity that is several hundred pages long) finally concludes that the best analogy is to say that the triune God is Lover, the Beloved, and the Love that binds them together. While it has been argued that this does not put the Holy Spirit on the same footing as the others, Augustine's analogy has the advantage of highlighting the relational and dynamic character of the Trinity: God is not three static "things" or even three "beings." God *is* a dynamic relationship or relatedness, the activity of Lover-Beloved-Love. Augustine goes on to say that creation is the result of the overflowing or superabundance of the love among the three persons of God.

One of the more important implications of the doctrine of the Trinity is the way in which it reinterprets the ideas of unity and diversity. In ordinary experience, unity often is thought to mean uniformity. One way we express unity with others is to wear uniforms: from military uniforms to the paraphernalia of one's favorite sports team, wearing similar clothing reinforces a sense of identity and community with others. It also serves to differentiate between insiders and outsiders, "us" and "them." In the same way, difference often serves to divide. We tend to stereotype others based on how they are different from us, using categories such as race, gender, age, economic status, sexual orientation, religion, language, and physical characteristics. The triune vision of God goes against both of these common experiences. In this way of understanding the triune God, unity does not demand uniformity, and difference does not frustrate oneness. God is really one *and* three; really united and really different at the same time.

How might this view of who God is assist us in thinking about religious diversity? Rather than being a stumbling block to Christian thinking about this question, might this very idea of God contain clues to help us understand the plurality of human religious experience and expression? At least two theologians working on this question have proposed answers to these questions. While their approaches and conclusions are quite different, they both begin with the important idea at the heart of the idea of the triune God, namely, the coexistence of unity and diversity. If God is both one *and* really diverse *at the same time*, does this not suggest that the same might be true of the way God relates to humanity? Might the idea that God is one and also three suggest that God can be experienced by human beings in markedly different ways and still be the same God?

In fact, this is one way to account for and interpret the diversity among Christians. As suggested above, Christians have long been tempted to practice various forms of "unitarianism" of one person of the Trinity over the others. Some branches of the church, for example, have emphasized the sovereignty of God and concentrated their attention on God as Creator and Father. Others have been centered in devotion to Christ, understood, for example, as seeking unity with Christ in the Eucharist or presenting Christian faith as a "personal relationship with Jesus." For still others, the most important way of experiencing God is through the Holy Spirit. For most Christians, this is a matter of piety, devotion, or experience. Emphasis on one person of the Trinity does not lead to a denial of the other two. Rather, individuals have been drawn to, and communities have been formed around, distinctive ways of experiencing one aspect of the triune God.

If this is one way to understand the diversity among Christians, can a similar argument provide an analogy through which to understand the diversity of religious life? Can the God who has revealed Godself to be a "unity in diversity" also relate to others in distinct and diverse ways? One theologian who uses this as the basis for accounting for religious diversity is S. Mark Heim.[3] He grounds his argument in the "unity in diversity" of God and contends that this view of God opens the door to understanding the nature of reality and of "truth" in such a way that one can account for the multiplicity of religious experience and expression. Heim is a Christian theologian with years of experience in Christian ecumenical and interreligious dialogue. He begins by insisting that Christians must take seriously the real religious differences between and among the religions of the world. Heim is critical of the kind of pluralism that posits a simplistic many-paths-up-one-mountain view in such a way that it minimizes religious differences. But he is just as critical of exclusivism that automatically writes off any view of God except one's own.

Heim begins with the recognition that the world's religions think about God and the human condition in very different ways. These differences in fundamental views lead to what Heim describes as a multiplicity of "religious ends"—different ways of understanding the whole point of religious life. Thus it is a mistake to say that other religions seek salvation in someone or something other than Jesus as "Savior," because "salvation" is the distinctively *Christian* end. Salvation is the way Christians (but not necessarily others) understand and articulate the goal of faith or the religious life. To return to the analogy of many paths, Heim argues that not only are the paths of the religions different; the "ends" to which they believe they are going are just as different.

It may be helpful, to understand Heim's argument, to think about planning a trip from Chicago to the West Coast. One might begin in Chicago and follow roughly the old Route 66, south across Illinois and Missouri, down to Oklahoma, pick up Interstate 40 crossing the panhandle of Texas into northern

New Mexico and Arizona, ending up in Los Angeles. Or one might take Interstate 80 across Illinois and Iowa, Nebraska and Wyoming, and then from Salt Lake City to San Francisco. Or one might take Interstate 90 or 94 across South or North Dakota (respectively), through Montana and Idaho, and end up in Seattle. From one point of view, we have described many paths that end up at one destination, the West Coast. Anyone who has lived in any of those cities, however, will be quick to point out that Seattle and San Francisco are decidedly *not* Los Angeles. These are really different destinations, and the difference really matters both to the people who live there and to the traveler.

Heim argues that the doctrine of the Trinity allows Christians to take two approaches to religious diversity. First of all, the Trinity reminds Christians that while Christian faith is inexplicably tied to the person and work of Jesus Christ, Christian faith is also more than Christ. Thus Christians can account for the presence of God in the lives of others as we have here: through the doctrine of creation or through the universal presence and activity of the Spirit. But Heim wants to go further than this. He argues that the diversity within the being of God opens the way to think about both truth and reality in such a way that what appear to be "different truths" may be true simultaneously. This point is in fact clear in Trinitarian doctrine. The doctrine of the Trinity claims that God the Son is incarnate; God the Father is not. This leads to the recognition that we hold two things to be true that appear almost contradictory. We say that God becomes flesh, is born and dies, *and* that God is infinite and eternal, without form, not confined to time or space. Each of these is a distinct truth claim. Christian faith argues that each of these "contradictories" is true within the unity in diversity that is the triune God.

Heim argues that this distinctive way of holding very different understandings of God together serves as a way to understand different religious ends. What if, he posits, the nature of reality is such that more than one religious path and "end" work? What if (as seems to be the case) there is more than one way to account for reality and the human condition, and more than one way to live the "good life"? All that is required is that reality be constituted in such a way that these multiple under-standings can be sustained, that is, that they "work" for those who hold them. Why would God structure the universe this way? The answer appeals to the natural world in which we find great variety in the ways in which plant and animal life respond to the diversity of habitat and location. Out of a "plenitude" of grace (the "overflowing love" of the triune God, to return to Augustine's metaphor) God desires many rather than just one form of the good life.

A very different approach to the Trinity as the foundation for a theological understanding of religious diversity comes from Jacques Dupuis, a Jesuit scholar who has lived and taught theology for many years in India. Dupuis uses the Trinity as one of several theological approaches to religious diversity, but where Heim sees the possibility of multiple "ends," Dupuis emphasizes the universal "salvific" will of God that operates in, with, and among all the religious expressions of humankind. What Christians know is God's self-disclosure in Jesus Christ as Savior of all. Christians can and must proclaim this "truth," while also recognizing that this is not all or the only truth of God. Thus Christians can learn about other forms of God's presence through the religious testimony of others.

In Christian theology we sometimes talk about the "eco-nomic" as distinguished from the "immanent" Trinity. Accord-ing to this understanding, while the three persons are truly one within the being of God (the "immanent" reality), we can at the same time distinguish between the persons based on their relationship to us and the world (the "economic" reality). So, while creation is the "work" of all three (for God is one), we call God the Father "Creator" or "Maker of heaven and earth." And while all share in the work of redemption, Christ is rightly called "Redeemer." And while all participate in giving gifts for the living of the Christian life, the Spirit is called "Sustainer." Dupuis uses this as an analogy through which to talk about God having multiple ways of working in the lives of humanity across time and cultures. The important point that Dupuis brings to this discussion is to remind us of the fundamental Christian conviction that it is not the different religious paths that save people; it is God alone who saves. Thus, he wants to reorient the question, from asking about the validity (or lack of it) of other traditions to focusing on what Christians can legitimately say about how God is at work in a variety of ways to accomplish God's will and work. This work, as Dupuis sees it, is the ultimate redemption or reconciliation of all creation. Once again, preserving the distinctively Trinitarian value of unity and diversity enables this theologian to account both for God's truth in the Christian revelation and God's activity in the life of humankind.[4]

In this brief discussion, we cannot begin to do justice to the complexity and subtlety of the thought of these two theologians. Both are examples of creative theological reflection deeply grounded in the core of Christian faith that provides for a way to understand the goodness of God and to account for the real diversity among the religious expressions of God's people. What is important about these contributions is that they find ways to understand religious diversity without sacrificing the core of Christian thought. In various ways, these interpretations turn on the doctrine of the Holy Spirit, who is at one and the same time the Spirit of Jesus Christ and the manifestation of God's presence in all of life. This way of understanding Christian faith affirms that the Spirit will always do what Christ does—namely, save, heal, or redeem—but that the Spirit will not be limited in accomplishing this work to those who follow Christian faith. The wind indeed blows where it (that is to say, where God the Spirit) wills.

Thus far, I have attempted to show a trajectory of biblical and theological interpretation that holds together the universality of divine love with the particularity of confessing Jesus Christ as the full expression of that love. In the next chapter I will summarize the approaches explored thus far and consider the practical implications of this positive account of religious diversity for the mission and witness of the church.

5

A Wideness in God's Mercy

We return to the question that is the occasion of the book: How will Christians live in a multifaith world? The question is both theological and practical. From a theological perspective, the answer must be rooted in our understanding of who God is and of God's purposes in the world. From a practical perspective, we must weigh the consequences of our answers in terms of what they mean not only for us but for the others who also live in this society and culture.

The theological question is, how are Christians to understand the presence and continuing vitality of other religious traditions in the world today in light of our understanding of God revealed in Jesus Christ? The practical question is, how are Christians to live in a democratic nation that is committed to freedom of religious thought and expression and is now a very diverse nation religiously? In theological reflection, context matters. Many Christians live in social and political situations very different from those of us in the United States, where religious freedom is constitutionally guaranteed. Some Christians find themselves in places where they are a minority religion, perhaps subject to threat from others. These differences in context shape both the experience of Christian faith and how the question of religious diversity is understood. This reflection is written in light of the strong Christian tradition and increasing religious diversity that we experience today in American culture.

The continuing vitality of non-Christian religious traditions suggests to many Christians that the work of evangelism is far from done. There are souls to be saved and lives to be won for Christ. They believe that the primary task of Christians is to make as many disciples as possible, to share God's love with the world, and to bring the good news to all, even if the faithful in other religions believe they are following a divine leading in their own tradition. Some Christians add to this evangelical commitment the belief that the existence of other religious traditions is in fact evidence of the work of Satan in the world, drawing people away from the true God to the worship of idols. From this they conclude that Christians need to limit (or even, perhaps, eliminate) the practice of other religions while at the same time attempting to convert to the Christian faith those who follow other traditions.

My intent in this book has been to suggest that this is not the only way to understand either Christianity or other religions. There is another way to account for religious diversity. This way opens up distinctly different ways for Christians to relate to those of other faiths, even as we find ourselves living in a society characterized by rich religious diversity. What are the convictions that underlie the view that Christianity is not the only "true" religion? The review of the biblical story in previous chapters leads to a set of theological convictions that lay the foundation for Christians living in a multifaith world.

First, Christians assume that all humanity is one family, because all are children of one Creator. Second, our tradition suggests that God made covenant with all humankind before the division into cultures, languages, and religious traditions and that this covenant commits both God and human beings to the preservation of life. These convictions lead, third, to an ethic of mutual respect. If all human beings are in fact one family, and if the Creator has commanded us to preserve life, then it follows that we are obligated to live with all others respecting their dignity, integrity, and individuality. I would argue that this means respecting their religious life as well and will say more below about what this means in practice.

The affirmation of the universal love of God is one truth. Alongside it stands another truth, and unless these two truths stand together, the identity of Christian faith is compromised. The second theological affirmation is that Jesus Christ is Savior and Lord. For Christians, the universal love of God is made explicit and comes to life in Jesus. This is what we mean when we confess that Jesus is the Son of God or God *incarnate*, literally, God in the flesh. Christians confess that through the life, death, and resurrection of Jesus, God is at work to reconcile humanity with God. Salvation through Christ is thus the distinctively Christian "religious end" or way of understanding God's purposes in the world. But this cannot be construed in such a way as to invalidate or negate God's covenant to love, preserve, and sustain all of life.

This leads to an open question: given that God *does* indeed reveal Godself in the person and work of Jesus Christ, is that the *only* way that God discloses Godself or relates to humankind? Put another way: given that salvation *is* the work God is doing in the world, is salvation through Christ the *only* work that God is about? The principle of God's universal love for all suggests that a more open answer might be made to these questions without violating God's real presence in Christ. At the very least, if salvation is God's work and God's alone, then we should be prepared to imagine that God can and will accomplish this purpose in God's own ways. To support this view, I have argued that we consider again the work of God the Holy Spirit, everywhere the giver and renewer of life.

Finally, the doctrine of the triune nature of God provides a way in which to understand how unity and real diversity can be understood as deeply compatible. As the unity and diversity within God's own being is a potential metaphor for understanding the diversity of human culture, so we continue to wonder, does it provide a basis for understanding the diversity of human religious life?

What I have tried to present here is a range of possibilities for viewing positively this diversity of human religious life in light of who Christians believe God to be. The fact that the human family follows many and very different religious traditions may be part of God's purpose. I have attempted to show that there is room in the biblical witness for a positive appraisal of religious diversity and for affirming life in community with those who follow other traditions.

When we begin with the view that all of life is in the hands of a generous and life-giving God, then we are led to ask whether today's experience of religious diversity might be part of God's own providential ordering of creation. Put another way, can God's design for us and the world be found in this context in which we find ourselves as committed Christians newly aware of the interreligious reality of that world? Has God brought us to this situation in order to help us understand Christian faith in renewed and deeper ways? If so, how are we as Christians called to live in this new situation? As the nineteenth-century poet James Russell Lowell wrote, "New occasions teach new duties."

LIVING WITH RELIGIOUS DIVERSITY

What "new duties" might arise from the positive assessment of religious diversity as part of God's work in the world, not to mention in our American context? I believe we can identify six practical consequences for Christian life and faith.

1. Christians are called to have humility with respect to the question of religious truth.
2. We are called to treat others with respect, rather than simply with "tolerance."
3. Christians should give greater attention to the "practices" of Christian faith and how those practices make for a "Christian shape" to life in the world today.

4. We must understand what the Christian practice of "bearing witness" to our faith or relationship with Jesus Christ means in a multifaith world.
5. Christians are called to "work with others for justice, freedom, and peace," which has significant implications for building civil community.
6. Christians are called to engage others in dialogue with the goal of learning and being open to transformation in the process.

1. HUMILITY WITH RESPECT TO TRUTH

The first "new duty" to which Christians are called is to approach the question of religious truth with humility. This is probably the most controversial of the six challenges, for Christianity has historically put significant emphasis on theological doctrines and asserted that these doctrines make truth claims about reality. As I noted in chapter 1, a distinctive aspect of Christian faith is the practice of theological reflection and the formulation of statements of belief or faith. This has led Christians in turn to define some ideas as "orthodox" and others as "heretical" or false.

I am not suggesting that the practice of attempting to state clearly what one believes and why is in and of itself problematic. Rather, the problem comes when the church or individuals within it come to think that theological statements can be made with ultimate certainty or finality. In fact, a significant difference of opinion exists on this topic within Christianity itself. The Roman Catholic and Orthodox traditions have given great authority to church councils and to the teaching office of the church. Considerable confidence is placed in those bodies to provide authoritative interpretations of Christian faith. Protestants have argued (at least in principle) that church councils, because they are made up of human beings, are always subject to error. Church teaching and the work of theologians are also in principle always open to "reformation," renewal, and correction over time. In practice, however, Protestants have often been just as certain as Roman Catholics and Orthodox about their ability to state definitively what is true or false with respect to Christian doctrine.

The issue of the nature of religious truth is not being raised for the first time by the debate over religious diversity. This question has a long history in Christian theology. Both the Bible and Christian tradition provide at least three reasons why Christians might be modest with respect to how we understand theological truth claims. First, the Bible is not a book of doctrine or an attempt to lay out religious "ideas." The Bible is fundamentally a narrative with liturgical and poetic writings. Even the letters of the New Testament, which come the closest to being an exposition of theological ideas, are often worked out in the context of specific church problems or issues. Most Christian theology is extrapolation from biblical material, and down through the centuries the very variety of that material has led to some of the most significant theological debates among Christians. Theology is, therefore, often called "second order" speech. The word of God in the person of Christ and in Scripture is "first order." If theological ideas are thus understood as *human* reflection on what is revealed in Scripture, it seems appropriate to conclude that such ideas should not be understood as conveying "absolute truth," but rather as attempts to understand and express the truth of God as humans can comprehend it at a given point in time.

Theological ideas will necessarily be conditioned by the context and limitations of those who formulate them. Numerous examples can be given of the way in which Christian thinking about deeply important issues has evolved over time. For example, during the time when slavery was practiced in the United States, white Christians often argued that Africans were descendants of Ham, the cursed son of Noah, and therefore "deserved" their status as chattel slaves. Such a view is now clearly seen as a hideous misuse of Scripture. In a similar way, Christians for centuries read statements in the Gospels in a way that led them to call Jewish neighbors "Christ killers." Rejecting this view is not a matter of great religious "tolerance." It is the recognition that what was once taught as religious truth was based on a serious misreading of Scripture and on a misrepresentation of God's will.

This leads directly to another reason for being cautious about how to understand religious truth. Theology is literally "talk about God." Embedded in the very notion of God is the understanding that human beings will never be able to comprehend God fully. God is Creator; we are creatures. The finite creature is by definition less than the infinite Creator. "My thoughts are not your thoughts, nor are your ways my ways," as the prophet Isaiah put it (55:8). This is the real source of religious humility: the recognition that we are not God and that our ideas about God will never be complete until God brings all things to completion. "Now I know only in part," Paul wrote (1 Cor. 13:12). This is the stance with which Christians should approach any question about who God is and what God is up to in the world. We can indeed say that we know "truth" about God; what humans can never say is that we know "the whole truth and nothing but the truth."

Finally, the issue of truth versus falsehood is a distinctly Western and in some ways peculiarly modern question. Since the European Enlightenment of the eighteenth century, we have become accustomed to thinking that truth is something that can be demonstrated or for which there is clear and compelling evidence. Something is true if it can be verified or confirmed in some way; if it cannot, we say it is false. This leads to the idea that truth rules out contradictions; if one thing is true, then others are necessarily false. For example, if it is true that it is day, then it follows that it is not night. Unless, of course, it is dawn or twilight, and therein lies the problem. Many aspects of human experience do not fit neatly into this type of truth-falsehood dichotomy, and religious experience is one of them. This is not to say that there is no such thing as religious truth, but rather that religious truth does not fit into the categories of truth-falsehood that work well in modern, scientific arenas. When people of faith talk about truth, we need to be careful not to confine our understanding of truth to this modern definition.

When Christians talk about truth with respect to faith, the best place to begin is that challenging verse from John 14: "I am the way, and the truth, and the life." What does it mean to claim that Jesus Christ is "truth"? One way to say this is that for Christians, truth is personal or is a person, namely, Jesus Christ himself. It is not ideas about Jesus that are true or false, but his own life, death, resurrection, and continuing presence that *is* truth. The truth of another person or the truth that a person is can only be known *personally*, that is to say, in the context of a personal relationship. I cannot know the truth of a person whom I do not know, and as I come to know another person, my understanding of the depth and nature of the truth about that person grows.

This approach to understanding what Christians mean by theological truth has been expressed by many people and in a variety of other contexts. The implications of this line of thinking for how Christians might live in a religiously pluralistic world are significant. If religious or theological truth is set free from the understanding that if one idea is true, all others must be false, the door has been opened for the possibility of more than one view of God and God's relationship to the world. We are then able to say, for example, that Jesus Christ is indeed Savior and Lord *and at the same time* God is still in covenant relationship with God's people Israel, who will be saved or redeemed through that covenant. That is precisely the argument that Paul makes in Romans 9–11. Both of these things are true, based on Paul's understanding of Scripture and his experience with Christ. Affirming one idea as truth does not require thinking of the other as falsehood. Rather, these are truths that, if you will, nest or are embedded in one another.

This is a somewhat straightforward example for Christians, based as it is on Scripture itself. As it is now widely acknowledged, Judaism and Christianity are sibling religions, each heirs of the same foundational story of God's covenant relationship with humanity. While each tradition has developed in distinctive ways, their shared foundation makes it easy to see this as a case of compatible (even if very different) religious truths. It remains to be seen how and whether such a case can or will be made with Islam and whether the three Abrahamic faiths can see one another as heirs of the same promise.

For Christians, this approach becomes more challenging with religious traditions that are very different—especially those that are not grounded in a personal view of God. But the important beginning point for the conversation is to agree that *affirming the truth of one tradition does not automatically require believing that all other religious ideas and traditions are false.* Further, to say that multiple religious ideas can be true at the same time does not mean that the one I hold is less true than if it were the one and only truth.

In fact, there is a good *Christian* theological reason for affirming that other religious traditions have within them truth about God. If God is the one in whose image all humanity has been created, and if we believe (as we claim) that God loves all that God has made, it follows that God has somehow been present to all people and has provided the means for relationships of various kinds. Therefore, Christians should expect to find evidence of the gracious presence and activity of God in the lives, cultures, and traditions of others . . . simply because of who we believe God to be. Humility with respect to truth leaves us open to gifts that might come to us from other parts of God's family.

2. RESPECT RATHER THAN TOLERANCE

In a world of multiple and diverse religious faiths, Christians are called to respect rather than merely tolerate those faiths and the people who practice them. Toleration, religious and otherwise, is an important civic virtue highly prized in American culture. It has allowed for a democratic political system to thrive in a nation made up of peoples from many nations and cultures. Religious toleration was what at least some of the

European colonists came to North America to seek and secure. But toleration can have a negative side to it. That is, it can easily be taken to mean: "I don't care what others do (or believe) as long as it doesn't bother me," which suggests a certain lack of care for or interest in one's neighbors. Toleration is a civic virtue, and an important one at that. But Christians should be invited to a greater level of interest in and concern for the well-being of their neighbors.

What, for example, does it mean "to love one's neighbor as oneself" when the neighbor is a Hindu or Buddhist? Some might argue that the best gift Christians can give is to share their faith in Christ. To them, fulfilling the love command means engaging in evangelization. But if we begin from the view that God is working in the lives of all people, that the Spirit is *everywhere* the giver and renewer of life, then we come to see that the religious identity of the other is likely to be as close to their sense of identity and personhood as Christian identity is to us. If the first or the only way we relate to our neighbors of other religions is by attempting to change their identity, we fail to respect the other as a child of God. Respecting the faith of others does not mean that we abandon evangelization, but it does have a great deal to do with how we conduct this part of the church's ministry.

Respect has to do with acknowledging the integrity of another person, rather than with the ideas that person holds; respect is not the same as agreement. To respect another is to acknowledge the other as a person whom God loves just as God loves me. It is to honor the value of the other's life. This is the foundation on which the "love command" is built: to respect the other is to work for the other's well-being as well as my own.

One practical implication of respect is that it leads Christians to work for laws and policies that provide the same protections of religious belief and practice for others that they provide for Christians. And it means that Christians will resist attempts to impose Christian observance and practice (even or perhaps especially in the watered-down form known as "civil religion") on others. Once again, this is not to advocate a secular version of tolerance, nor do I advocate the banishment of religion from public life. Rather, this is a concrete expression of the "golden rule" that we should do to others as we would have them do to us. Respect and love call upon us to seek the good for the other, and this includes what is good for their religious and spiritual life.

The United States Army presents a practical example of what this kind of respect looks like. Army chaplains are recruited from all religious traditions in American life, and all of them, of whatever denomination or tradition, are responsible to understand and provide care for soldiers in the soldiers' own tradition. An interesting extension of such a policy would be for public schools to provide instruction on all the religions that are practiced in the United States, including an introduction to holidays, songs, foods, and so on, particular to each tradition. This would help us move beyond what is now often presented as the only alternatives: observing only Christian holidays (because Christianity is the predominant tradition) or recognizing none at all.

3. RECOVERING CHRISTIAN PRACTICES

The third "new duty" to which Christians are called by virtue of living in a multifaith society is the recovery of Christian practices. For much of modern Protestant life, religious identity was sought in doctrine or right ideas. Presbyterians and Lutherans and Baptists each distinguished themselves by what they believed and did not believe and by how they differed, sometimes in highly technical ways, from one another. All celebrated the Lord's Supper, for example, but they argued strenuously about whether it is a sacrament or an ordinance, about whether Jesus is really present or simply remembered by faith, and so forth. But when we understand religion primarily as holding a set of theological or ideological ideas, we are in danger of losing much of what religion is and means for human life. It is important to love God with all our mind; and theology is a way to do that. But we are invited to love God with heart and soul and might, that is to say, with our whole being. Heart and soul and energy are engaged by what we call religious practices. They remind us that religion is not just something we think about; it is something we do.

Christians have developed a wide range of practices that nourish and express relationship with God. Christians pray, both privately and in gathered community. We celebrate special days and seasons as reminders of God's story with God's people. We read, study, and memorize Scripture. We give offerings to care for the needs of others and build hospitals, schools, and community centers to care for the needs of the body and mind as well as the spirit. We work for justice in society. The list goes on. It is important to recognize that there are many traditional ways in which Christians have practiced the faith, acting out our understanding of what relationship with God through Jesus Christ means for daily living.

There are several advantages to a renewed emphasis on practices of faith. First of all, it is simply more faithful to Christian tradition. When Christianity is thought of primarily as a set of religious ideas or theological doctrines, this ignores the wide range of artistic and musical expressions that Christians have developed to express and interpret the faith. Similarly, if being a Christian means little more than occasional (or even regular) Sunday worship attendance, we are likely to discover that this is simply not very satisfying. We will either get bored or begin to hunger for more. We have resources from two millennia of Christian life, if only we are willing to discover and use them.

Second, an emphasis on practices of faith can become a wonderful entry point into understanding and appreciating the faith of others. They help us to move from argument about whose religious ideas are right to a sympathetic knowledge of how we all live our faith day to day. Some years ago an official of a large Roman Catholic archdiocese was interviewed on the radio about the challenges of helping a traditionally ethnic parish welcome members of another ethnic group as they moved into the neighborhood. One predominantly Polish parish was experiencing a rapid influx of Spanish-speaking per-

sons, mostly from Mexico. There were arguments in the congregation between the two groups about how many masses to
have in which language and tensions about how the parish
should be run. After considerable study and dialogue, leaders
from the two groups discovered that Polish Catholics and Mexican Catholics share a deep love of parades and feasts to celebrate significant holy days. Pretty soon the feast day of Our
Lady of Guadalupe was featuring Polish food, and Mexican
bands were appearing at traditionally Polish celebrations.

This example from within one faith tradition might help us
to contemplate how understanding one's own religious practices
can lead to new and deeper relationships with others. When
faith traditions are considered from the vantage point of practices, rather than competing theological ideas, some intriguing
similarities emerge. For example, many religions involve organizing time: a day in the week that is set aside for worship, festi-
vals throughout the year that mark important events in the
tradition's history, seasons for reflection and celebration. Many
people have found that understanding or experiencing the tradition of another leads to deeper appreciation of one's own.
Much of Jewish life is centered in the home: the weekly Sabbath
meal and the annual celebration of Passover. Being invited to
share such meals with Jewish friends has led me to reflect on and
deepen my own practices of Sabbath keeping, of hospitality, and
of including others in festival meals at Christmas and Easter.

How and whether persons of varying religions can come
together for prayer or worship is a challenging and complex
issue. But a renewed understanding of religion as a set of practices and a renewed appreciation of Christian practices by
Christians can become a bridge to deeper appreciation of and
respect for others.

4. WITNESS AND EVANGELISM

The fourth "new duty" for Christians living in a multifaith world
is to continue to engage in witness and evangelism. Bearing

witness to the good news we know in Jesus Christ is one of the core Christian practices. The Great Commission was the church's first mission statement: "Go therefore and make disciples of all nations" (Matt. 28:19). In the Acts of the Apostles, this was precisely what happened. The disciples told the story of Jesus, and people received the news with joy and were baptized by the thousands (Acts 2:41). After his own conversion, Paul took up the ministry of preaching and organizing new communities of believers across the Mediterranean region. He made it as far as Rome and died hoping to journey on to Spain. Other apostles journeyed to India and Africa founding communities of Christians. Thousands followed in the footsteps of Paul and the early church, as Christian faith spread further into Africa and Europe. Missionary activity accompanied European exploration and colonization. In the nineteenth and twentieth centuries, American churches sent out thousands of missionaries to witness and to serve in the name of Jesus Christ. Telling others about Jesus Christ, sharing the faith, and inviting others to receive baptism and become members of the body of Christ are both historically and theologically at the core of Christian practice.

To some, this practice seems clearly at odds with life in a multifaith world. How can we respect the religious life of those who follow other religious traditions and bear witness to them at the same time? How is it possible to recognize the truth of God in the religious lives of others and at the same time attempt to convert them to Christian faith? These are particularly challenging questions for those of us who believe that God is already involved in the lives and cultures and (even if we cannot completely explain it) religions of all humankind.

The most obvious approach has been to emphasize ministries of compassion and community service as the most appropriate forms of Christian witness. To this end, Christians have built schools, hospitals, clinics, and orphanages. We have engaged in projects to provide clean water, sustainable farming, and even microbusiness, all in the name of helping one's neighbor as Christ commanded. All of these are important and necessary forms of Christian witness. They are expressions of the truth that faith will be known by its fruits. When such tangible forms of assistance and compassion are accompanied by words that explain how this work relates to how we understand God's love at work in Jesus Christ, then these are indeed appropriate expressions of the gospel to the world.

As important as those forms of ministry are, they beg the question of whether or not Christians are still called to "make disciples," that is, specifically to invite others to find faith in God through Jesus Christ. In fact, it is one of my Jewish colleagues, Professor Sarah Tanzer, who has regularly reminded me that this activity of "bearing witness" is part of the core identity of Christianity, and that to abandon it would be to take something essential away from what has made Christianity what it is.

In fact, living in today's multifaith world provides us an important opportunity to reconsider how witness and evangelism should be done. The theological principles we have discussed here have three practical implications for evangelization. First, we should make clear in our interaction with those from other traditions that we Christians assume that those with whom we speak are *already* beloved children of God: God cannot love them any more if they become Christian than God does now. Second, Christian proclamation should be ready to acknowledge the presence of God through the Holy Spirit already active and at work in the lives of others; Christians are not "bringing God to the godless" because God is present throughout all of God's creation. Third, Christian proclamation should be focused on the positive Christian vision: life now and eternally in communion (or right relationship) with God. Christian proclamation rooted in fear or threat (e.g., "if you die tonight, do you know where you will spend eternity?") is incompatible with the message of God's mercy and grace and God's sovereign freedom to save all whom God chooses. Salvation (union and communion with God) is God's gracious gift to the world in Jesus Christ. How God accomplishes this in the lives of individuals is finally a mystery; it is God who saves, not the messenger.

The motive for evangelization is also an important consideration. Christians bear witness to what God has done in Jesus Christ, on the one hand, in obedience to Christ's command. But we also bear witness, as Peter and John said to the religious authorities who wanted to put a stop to their preaching, because "we cannot keep from speaking about what we have seen and heard" (Acts 4:20). Christians bear witness because we cannot do otherwise. What God has done in Jesus Christ, for the world and in our own lives, is such a powerful and wonderful story that Christians are compelled to talk about it. In this sense, bearing witness is much like praise: both are ends in themselves. We tell the story of Jesus and we raise our voices in songs and prayers of praise because this is our grateful and joyous response to God's goodness. The effectiveness of Christian witness should be measured, then, not by how many converts are made, but by how authentically our testimony reports the good news. Telling the story is our job; redeeming or saving the world is God's, because salvation belongs to God alone.

5. WORKING TOGETHER FOR THE COMMON GOOD

The fifth "new duty" to which Christians are called in a multifaith world is to work together with others on projects and activities that advance the common good. As the most recent confessional statement of the Presbyterian Church put it, in a "broken and fearful world," the Holy Spirit empowers us "to work with others for justice, freedom and peace." When this statement was written, there was considerable discussion about the word "others." Shouldn't it read "other Christians" or even "other faithful people?" In the end, the decision was made that the word should stand, with all of the openness that it implies. Christians should be prepared to make common cause with any and all who seek to advance the cause of justice, freedom, and peace in our world. Once again, this is because we assume that this is God's work and that God can and will work through all persons to achieve those purposes. Jewish theologians have a term for this: *tikkun olan*, or the healing of the world; and noted Jewish scholars now argue in support of openness to embrace relationships with any and all who would share in this activity.

The first step we must take is for people from different faith traditions to come together to articulate the values and moral perspectives that are embedded in their own traditions and seek to discern where these values and perspectives are found in the traditions of others. A variety of enterprises have been working on this for some years. The World Council on Religion and Peace, for example, an international forum of religious leaders, is committed to identifying things that believers from different traditions can do together to bring peace. The Parliament of the World's Religions held in 1993 produced a document (although written primarily by Christian theologian Hans Küng) that was widely embraced as a statement of common vision for the welfare of humankind. This has now evolved into a permanent organization, the Council for the Parliament of the World's Religions, which has held international meetings in Cape Town and Barcelona drawing together people from all of the world's religious communities to continue the journey of getting to know one another and discerning ways to make common cause for peace and justice.[1] Within the United States, organizations like Habitat for Humanity have sought to bring together people of all faiths and no faith for the purpose of building safe, affordable housing for all. Calling it "the theology of the hammer," Habitat seeks to find common ground in the actual work of home building.

While there are certain values and ethical concerns that the religions do not share, there is real and growing consensus about many values, most notably the care of the poor, the protection of the environment, and the search for peace. Virtually all religious traditions teach care and concern for the poor, often enacted through the giving of alms or offerings. Some traditions, like Judaism, Islam, and Christianity, have ethical traditions that suggest enacting laws in society to guarantee food, clothing, and shelter as basic human rights or things necessary to the very dignity of the individual. Similarly, there is growing consensus that there are religious grounds to care for the natural world, whether as God's good creation or because of the right of all living things to life and prosperity.

Finally, and perhaps most urgent, is the commitment of religious leaders to the renunciation of violence as a means to achieve religious ends and to settle conflicts, religious and otherwise. Far too many conflicts in the world today are fueled by religious (as well as ethnic, cultural, and political) differences. While religion alone is rarely the sole cause of the conflict, it increases the hostility in far too many situations. The seemingly intractable conflicts in the Middle East involve challenging issues of land, nationalism, and control of natural resources. But the tensions among religious groups and the claims that they make exacerbate the level of emotion and response. Within all of the great religious traditions, including those implicated in the conflict in the Middle East, there is a strong tradition that renounces violence toward others and contends that peace is the way of God. If the religions of the world were to teach that we should respect those from other traditions and that the use of violence is morally and religiously wrong, people of faith would make a significant contribution to the well-being of the whole world. Christians might lead the way by renouncing violence as a means to resolving human problems, whether interpersonal or international.

6. INTERFAITH DIALOGUE

The last "new duty" to which Christians are invited is the discipline of learning from others about both ourselves and God. Many Christians have already done some of this through Christian ecumenical activities. Years of dialogue and participation in organizations such as councils of churches have reminded Christians that Christian faith is much bigger than any particular denominational expression. It has often been recognized that the various churches each bring specific gifts to the whole. For example, Episcopalians bring a rich love for liturgy and traditional worship; Presbyterians bring a tradition of serious scholarship and commitment to order and fairness in deliberative assemblies; those from historic African American churches bring a passion for preaching and for justice for the poor. The Roman Catholic Church has nurtured within itself wide varieties of spiritual practice and formation that are now more available to Protestants. This list is admittedly limited and depends on certain stereotypes of denominational life. But the experiences of ecumenical dialogue themselves have been rich and transformative and have had at least two results. First, participants have come to appreciate the variety of Christian life and been able to incorporate into their own life some of the gifts and practices of others. Second, most participants have come to a new understanding and appreciation of their own traditions and the gifts they have to offer to the wider church.

This kind of ecumenical experience is proving to be a model or analogy for interfaith conversations. While there is less common ground to begin with between traditions of different religions, the dynamic remains the same. A greater awareness of others and the way they understand and live their faith becomes an opportunity to see the broader scope of God's work and (at the same time) to be drawn more deeply into one's own tradition.

An intriguing example of this kind of interfaith activity is a program of dialogue and exchange between Christian and Buddhist monks and nuns. Begun in the 1960s and given prominence and leadership by Thomas Merton, Roman Catholic religious men and women from North America have held conferences and study sessions with counterparts from Buddhist monasteries in India and other parts of southeast Asia. Going beyond theory to practice, a program in "inter-monastic exchange" has enabled monks and nuns from both traditions to live for periods of time with the other in order to learn more about practices of meditation and prayer. Through this process of mutual discovery, women and men who understand themselves to be called to the contemplative life have come to recognize how similar and adaptable the practices of meditation are between Christian and Buddhist life. Despite profound differences in understandings of God and the nature of reality, the participants have discovered profound similarities in their core ethical values, especially the practice of hospitality and the commitment to peace. On neither side have these exchanges been the occasion for proselytism. Rather, they have led participants to profound discoveries about their own traditions and to a new understanding of the mystery of God's presence in the life of the world.[2]

Local congregations have long had a variety of interfaith programs that can become the occasion for deeper dialogue. In many cities interfaith services at Thanksgiving have brought religious leaders together in planning and leading worship. This could serve as the foundation for longer-term engagement, study, and mutual understanding. Individual Christian congregations sometimes develop relationships with synagogues or mosques that lead to genuine encounter and dialogue. The Fourth Presbyterian Church of Chicago and nearby Congregation Sinai have a long-standing relationship of this type. Fourth Church opens its sanctuary to the Jewish congregation for their services on the High Holy Days, and Congregation Sinai sponsors a Seder meal at Passover inviting Presbyterians to participate. A program of study about issues of peace in the Middle East and Bible study led by the pastor and rabbi have been well attended by members of both congregations. Conversations have been held about the possibility of a jointly sponsored trip to Israel-Palestine.

Dialogue experiences like this cannot be shared by everyone, but as the religious diversity increases in America, getting to know neighbors who come from other religious traditions is much more likely. For Christians, these encounters should be approached with both humility and confidence—with humility so as not to claim to know more about God than it is possible to know, and with confidence that we do in fact know God through the life, death, and resurrection of Jesus Christ. Such a stance allows both for honest and open engagement with the other and at the same time for continuing commitment to our

Christian way of being related to God. The result may not only serve the common good through mutual understanding; it may deepen our own faith at the same time.

CONCLUSION

In the story of Esther, the Jewish woman who becomes queen of Babylon during the exile, Mordecai appeals to Esther to intercede before the king on behalf of the Jews who are enduring persecution. Mordecai sends a message to Esther saying, "Who knows? Perhaps you have come to royal dignity for just such a time as this" (Esth. 4:14). As this study comes to an end, I have suggested some answers to the question of how Christians can understand our religiously diverse world in positive ways. But in the end, there are more questions to be asked and answered.

God's providence has brought us to this time and this place—as Christians in a multifaith world. Perhaps the continuing vitality of the many world religions is part of God's way of relating to and caring for all of God's human community. Perhaps this is our time as Christians to learn how to be Christians *and* (at the same time) to be neighbors and partners with those of other faiths. Perhaps what we call discipleship and what Jews call *tikkun olan* (the healing of the world) are deeply related and compatible. Perhaps truth about God and human life resides in us *and at the same time* in other traditions, because God is surely bigger than any one way of understanding and experiencing God. Perhaps we have been brought into such close relationship with people of other faiths so as to broaden our understanding and deepen our appreciation of the majesty and mystery of God. Perhaps this is our time as people of faith to respond to God's call for community and peace. Perhaps.

Notes

Preface

1. Wilfred Cantwell Smith, *The Faith of Other Men* (New York: Harper & Row, 1962), 132–33.
2. For a more thorough consideration of this approach to the Bible, see W. Eugene March, *The Wide, Wide Circle of Divine Love: A Biblical Case for Religious Diversity* (Louisville, KY: Westminster John Knox Press, 2005).
3. Presbyterian Church (U.S.A.), "A Brief Statement of Faith," in *The Book of Confessions* (Louisville, KY: Office of the General Assembly, 1991), 10.3 (lines 30–32) and 10.4 (line 71).

Chapter 1: Is This "My Father's" World or Not?

1. See especially Diana L. Eck, *A New Religious America: How a "Christian Country" Has Become the World's Most Religiously Diverse Nation* (San Francisco: HarperCollins, 2001).
2. See Veli-Matti Kaerkkaeinen, *An Introduction to the Theology of Religions: Biblical, Historical and Contemporary Perspectives* (Downers Grove, IL: InterVarsity Press, 2003).
3. For a discussion of this paradigm in approaching this issue of religious diversity, see Diana Eck, *Encountering God: A Spiritual Journey from Bozeman to Banaras* (Boston: Beacon Press, 1993).
4. Presbyterian Church (U.S.A.), *The Book of Confessions*, 7.170.
5. Austin Flannery, OP, ed., *Vatican Council II: The Basic Sixteen Documents* (Northport, NY: Costello Publishing Co., 1996), 571.
6. Clark H. Pinnock, *A Wideness in God's Mercy: The Finality of Jesus Christ in a World of Religions* (Grand Rapids: Zondervan Publishing House, 1992).
7. Presbyterian Church (U.S.A.), *The Study Catechism* [approved by the 210th General Assembly (1998)], http://www.pcusa.org/catech/studycat.htm.

8. A number of books provide surveys and critiques of various approaches to religious diversity. Among the most helpful are Paul Knitter, *Introducing Theologies of Religions* (Maryknoll, NY: Orbis Books, 2002) and Jacques Dupuis, SJ, *Toward a Christian Theology of Religious Pluralism* (Maryknoll, NY: Orbis Books, 2001).

Chapter 2: Many Faiths—One Family

1. Irving Greenberg, *For the Sake of Heaven and Earth: The New Encounter between Judaism and Christianity* (Philadelphia: Jewish Publication Society, 2004), 57.
2. I am indebted to my colleague Theodore Hiebert for this reading of the Babel narrative.
3. Theodore Hiebert, ed., *Toppling the Tower: Essays on Babel and Diversity* (Chicago: McCormick Theological Seminary, 2004), 10.
4. Amy-Jill Levine, "Ruth," in *The Women's Bible Commentary*, ed. Carol A. Newsome and Sharon H. Ringe (Louisville, KY: Westminster/John Knox Press, 1992), 79.
5. See James L. Kugel, *The Bible As It Was* (Cambridge, MA: Belknap Press, 1997), 123–30.

Chapter 3: At the Name of Jesus

1. For an overview of Christian theological approaches to the issue of religious diversity, see Veli-Matti Karkkainen, *An Introduction to the Theology of Religions: Biblical, Historical and Contemporary Perspectives*.
2. Beverly Roberts Gaventa, *The Acts of the Apostles,* Abingdon New Testament Commentaries (Nashville: Abingdon Press, 2003), 94.
3. *Vatican Council II: The Basic Sixteen Documents*, 574.
4. Ibid., 22.
5. Terrance L. Tiessen, *Who Can Be Saved? Reassessing Salvation in Christ and World Religions* (Downers Grove, IL: InterVarsity Press, 2004).
6. Presbyterian Church (U.S.A.), *The Study Catechism*, question 49.

Chapter 4: Everywhere That We Can Be

1. Gaventa, *The Acts of the Apostles*, 142.
2. *The Book of Confessions*, 10.4.

3. S. Mark Heim, *The Depth of the Riches: A Trinitarian Theology of Religious Ends* (Grand Rapids: Eerdmans, 2001). See also his earlier work *Salvations: Truth and Difference in Religion* (Maryknoll, NY: Orbis Books, 1995).

4. See Jacques Dupuis, SJ, *Toward a Christian Theology of Religious Pluralism* and *Christianity and the Religions: From Confrontation to Dialogue* (Maryknoll, NY: Orbis Books, 2002).

Chapter 5: A Wideness in God's Mercy

1. Information about these organizations can be found at their websites: www.wcrp.org and www.cpwr.org.

2. For more information about the Monastic Interreligious Dialogue, see www.monasticdialog.com.

For Further Reading

D'Costa, Gavin. *The Meeting of Religions and the Trinity.* Maryknoll, NY: Orbis Books, 2000.

Dupuis, SJ, Jacques, *Toward a Christian Theology of Religious Pluralism.* Maryknoll, NY: Orbis Books, 1997.

Eck, Diana. *Encountering God: A Spiritual Journey from Bozeman to Banaras.* Boston: Beacon Press, 1993.

Heim, S. Mark. *The Depth of Riches: A Trinitarian Theology of Religious Ends.* Grand Rapids: Eerdmans, 2001.

———. *Salvations: Truth and Difference in Religion.* Maryknoll, NY: Orbis Books, 1995.

Hutchison, William R. *Religious Pluralism in America: The Contentious History of a Founding Ideal.* New Haven, CT: Yale University Press, 2003.

Knitter, Paul F. *Introducing Theologies of Religions.* Maryknoll, NY: Orbis Books, 2002.

March, W. Eugene. *The Wide, Wide Circle of Divine Love.* Louisville, KY: Westminster John Knox Press, 2004.

Netland, Harold. *Encountering Religious Pluralism: The Challenge to Christian Faith and Mission.* Downers Grove, IL: InterVarsity Press, 2001.

Pinnock, Clark H. *A Wideness in God's Mercy: The Finality of Jesus Christ in a World of Religions.* Grand Rapids: Zondervan Publishing House, 1992.

Sacks, Jonathan. *The Dignity of Difference: How to Avoid the Clash of Civilizations.* Rev. ed. London: Continuum, 2003.

Samartha, Stanley J. *One Christ—Many Religions: Toward a Revised Christology.* Maryknoll, NY: Orbis Books, 1991.

Smith, Wilfred Cantwell. *The Faith of Other Men.* New York: Harper & Row, 1962.

Suchocki, Marjorie Hewitt. *Divinity & Diversity: A Christian Affirmation of Religious Pluralism.* Nashville: Abingdon Press, 2003.

Scripture Index

Subject Index

Abel, 31
Abraham
  as common ancestor of Jews,
    Muslims, and Christians, 6, 30,
    88–89
  covenant between God and, 28,
    36, 37, 38, 40, 50
  descendants of, 29
  faith of, 60
  and Hagar and Ishmael, 30
  in heaven, 51
  and Melchizedek, 31
  Paul on, 60
Africa, 45, 94
African American churches, 99
African court official, 67–68, 71
Air Force Academy, U.S., 4
apologetic theology, 70, 71
Army, U.S., 91
Asenath, 30
Assyria, 41
Athens, 69–70
Augustine, 74

Babel, tower of, 25–28, 39–40
Babylon, 29
baptism
  of Jesus Christ, 66
  and Trinity, 74
Barth, Karl, 54
bearing witness, 93–96
Benedict XVI, Pope, 9–10
Bible
  as "first order" speech, 86
  focus of, 21, 86
  Ibn Ezra's style of exegesis for,
    26–27

and Protestants, 6–7
study and memorization of, 92
and theology, 86
See also New Testament; Old
  Testament
Bill of Rights, U.S., 17
Boaz, 31
"Brief Statement of Faith" (Presby-
  terian Church), ix, 72
Buddhism, 2, 3–4, 34, 45, 99–100

Calvin, John, 6, 54
Calvinism, 11
Canaanites, 52, 55
castration, 67
Catholic Church
  and authority of church councils
  and teaching office of church,
    85
  and ethnic differences, 92–93
  and inclusivism, 14
  on Jesus Christ, 9–10
  and non-Christians, 14, 56–57
  relationship between Jews, Mus-
    lims, and, 9–10
  on salvation, 14, 56–57
  and Second Vatican Council, 14,
    56–57
  and "special" versus "general"
    revelation, 54
  and spiritual practice and
    formation, 99
  and theology, 7
  as "true" church, 9
  See also Christianity
Christ. See Jesus Christ; New
  Testament